W9-CMT-081

JEWISH ENCOUNTERS

Jonathan Rosen, General Editor

Jewish Encounters is a collaboration between Schocken and
Nextbook, a project devoted to the promotion of Jewish literature, culture, and ideas.

>nextbook

PUBLISHED

FORTHCOMING

Hillel

RABBI JOSEPH TELUSHKIN

HILLEL

If Not Now, When?

NEXTBOOK · SCHOCKEN · NEW YORK

Schocken Books and colophon are registered trademarks of
Random House, Inc.

Library of Congress Cataloging-in-Publication Data
Telushkin, Joseph, [date]
    Hillel : if not now, when? / Joseph Telushkin.
    p. cm.
    Includes bibliographical references and index.
    ISBN 978-0-8052-4281-2
    1. Hillel, 1st cent. B.C./1st cent. A.D.—Teachings.
    2. Jewish ethics. 3. Beth Hillel and Beth Shammai.
    I. Title.
BM502.3.H55T45 2010
296.1'20092—dc22   2010008277

www.schocken.com
Printed in the United States of America
First Edition
2 4 6 8 9 7 5 3 1

If not now, when?

—HILLEL, *Ethics of the Fathers* 1:14

CONTENTS

Contents

Part III
Hillel and Jesus

Part IV
Lessons from the First Century
for the Twenty-first Century—and Beyond

INTRODUCTION

I was sitting with a rabbinic friend swapping stories about our lives and our work. He started talking about an encounter he recently had: "A Jewish man, probably in his early thirties, and his non-Jewish girlfriend came to speak with me. They want to marry, but his parents are dead set against their only son marrying a Gentile. I asked the woman what she thought about the parents' attitude, and she was honest. She said it seemed primitive and ridiculous. But she also said that, if necessary, she'd be willing to convert. After all, she wants to be a good person, and Judaism, she assumes, wants people to be good and might well have something to teach her about goodness. That's how she put it, 'might well have something to teach her about goodness.'"

"And what did you tell her?" I asked.

My friend, a rather traditional rabbi, answered: "I told her that we're in no rush to bring people in, that conversion to Judaism is a not a quick business: 'Presto, you're a Jew.' There's a lot to study, a lot of rituals to learn, and I certainly can't convert you before you do all that studying and commit yourself to practicing all that you study."

"And what did she say to that?"

"It was the boyfriend who spoke up. He seemed really

annoyed. 'I told you this was pointless,' he said to the girl, and then he turned to me. "We're getting married in six weeks, Rabbi. With or without your help."

My friend shrugged. "I told them that even if the two of them had come in with a more open attitude, six weeks was way too quick to do a conversion. Six months would be a stretch. They walked out with a book I gave them, but they're not coming back, I can tell." My friend shook his head a few times, his expression a mixture of sadness and annoyance. "What I was really thinking was that they'd be better off going to city hall and just getting their license. We don't need converts like that. One day, if she's interested in becoming a real Jew, she can come see me." He shrugged and regarded my skeptical face. "I know, I know, that day's never going to come."

I was quiet a minute, thinking about, of all things, a Talmudic sage who lived two thousand years ago named Hillel, and about an American-Jewish community that's been getting smaller and smaller, and whose members have been intermarrying at a rate of 40 percent and higher for more than thirty years.

"What about that comment she made to you?" I finally asked him.

He looked puzzled. "Which comment?"

"That Judaism might well have something to teach her about being a good person."

"Nice words," he conceded. "But I would have been a little more encouraged if she had actually said something about religion. Like maybe she had read about Shabbat and wanted to observe it. Or she was willing to keep kosher. At least then I would have felt that I had something to work with. But this couple gave me nothing to work with."

Nothing to work with. His words reverberated in my head.

At the time, I had already begun thinking that I would like to write a book about Hillel, and this encounter only heightened my resolve. Hillel, I am convinced, would have found absolutely wrongheaded my friend's all-too-common and reflexively discouraging approach to conversion. In the same way, I find it hard to imagine Hillel approving of the strange limbo in which some three hundred thousand Russians of questionable Jewish—and sometimes non-Jewish— parentage are presently living in Israel, many of whom want to become Jews. I thought of Hillel because he is not only, arguably, Judaism's greatest rabbinic sage, but also its most fearlessly inclusive.

He is also the rabbinic figure most willing to give ethical behavior equal—or even greater—weight, along with strict adherence to the ritual laws. The story for which Hillel is best known, a story we will look at in greater detail in this book, involves a non-Jew who is open to converting to Judaism but who wishes to learn about Judaism not in six weeks, but while "standing on one foot"—that is, in a single sound bite. Having literally been driven away with a stick by another rabbi who is affronted by his request, the non-Jew comes to Hillel, who is open to converting him. Hillel offers the man a single precept that surprisingly mentions neither God nor the rituals of the Torah, only the decent treatment of one's fellow man, along with the admonition to keep studying. If there is an essence of Hillel, it is in this story, in which he himself dares to offer an essence of Judaism.

Writing a conventional biography of Hillel is, alas, impossible. All that we know of Hillel's life comes from a variety of stories in the Talmud (and in related works, such as the Midrash). The Talmud is, along with the Bible, Judaism's most important literary creation, a compendium of legal discussions,* interpretations of the Bible, and an attempt to decipher what it is that God wants of human beings. Add to this folklore, ethical maxims, and stories, many of them about the Talmud's greatest rabbis. The Talmud was edited around the year 500 C.E.,† but its roots reach down to the oldest stratum of Judaism and, in the belief of the Talmud's sages, many of its teachings go back to Mount Sinai itself. But though a formal biography is impossible, for reasons that will soon become apparent, I believe it is still possible to construct a very clear impression of a man whose message speaks more urgently to Jews and Judaism today than that of any other Jewish figure in the last two thousand years.

Unfortunately, however, when it comes to details, we have considerably more biographical information about some of Judaism's far more ancient figures. In the case of Moses, the preeminent figure of the Hebrew Bible, we

---

* Sometimes we are told what the final ruling is, but often we are not.
† I am writing here of the Babylonian Talmud. The shorter and somewhat less authoritative Jerusalem Talmud (the *Yerushalmi*) was edited about a century earlier.

know how he met his wife, the names of his sons, his father, mother, brother, and sister, even the story of a certain measure of ill will that Miriam and Aaron, his siblings, felt toward him at one point in the desert wanderings.

The character who figures most prominently in the early books of the biblical prophets is Israel's second king, David. The son of Jesse, he is the youngest of eight brothers. We know the story of his first love, Michal; indeed, she is the only woman in the Bible whose love for a man is recorded ("Now Michal daughter of Saul had fallen in love with David"). We even know the story of the fight that led to the end of whatever love remained in their sad marriage (2 Sam. 6:16–23).

We move forward now to Hillel, perhaps the greatest rabbi of the Talmud. Hillel lived some twelve hundred years after Moses and about nine hundred years after David, and we should possess considerably more biographical information about him and his background than about theirs. But we don't. A Talmudic passage refers to him as "Hillel the Babylonian," from which we deduce that he was born in Babylon and subsequently came to Israel. The Talmud informs us that he went on to serve as *nasi*, the foremost religious leader of the community. Elsewhere, the Talmud traces his ancestry to King David, a touch of royalty that befits a man whose descendants would hold positions of religious leadership within the Jewish community for more than four hundred years. But we don't know the names of his father or mother or, for that matter, his wife (though the rabbis tell a story that reveals her to have been a highly sensitive practitioner of charity). We know the name of one son, Shimon—we don't know whether he had other children—and of his brother, Shebna, who is identified as a merchant. And because of the leadership roles many of Hillel's descendants assume, we know their names. Among them are four Gamliels, two additional Shimons, three Yehudahs, and the final leader, known as Hillel the Second.[1] We also know of the contemporaneous rabbi, Shammai—founder of his own school and the man who drove the would-be convert away— with whom Hillel and his disciples had numerous legal disputes. Surprisingly, however, there is only one story in which the two men actually appear together (*Shabbat* 17a). Nevertheless, they are a famous emblematic pair of adversaries who each uphold principles essential to Jewish tradition.*

We also know that Hillel was a disciple of two rabbis, Shmaya and Avtalion, who were the religious leaders of their age, and who were both descended from converts to Judaism. We know that Hillel assumed his position of leadership during a period of great instability and ignorance in Jewish life, in all likelihood related to the megalomaniacal kingship of Herod, who persecuted many of the era's religious teachers. While the Talmud ascribes to Hillel a life span of 120 years (as was the case with Moses), it would seem that his years of religious leadership ranged from approximately 30 B.C.E. to 10 C.E., which would mean this book is being published,

---

* And, of course, Jews are reminded of Hillel each year at the Passover seder, when they eat the famous sandwich he created, consisting of matzah, the bitter herb, and *charoset*, the mortar-like substance that symbolizes the mortar the Israelite slaves were required to produce for their Egyptian masters.

coincidentally, on what is possibly the two thousandth anniversary of his passing.

What we do possess about Hillel are many stories—stories scattered throughout the Talmud and Midrash along with many of his legal rulings and those of his disciples (*Beit Hillel*, the School of Hillel) that are recorded in the Mishnah, the Tosefta, and both the Jerusalem and the Babylonian editions of the Talmud.* It is from these stories and rulings that Hillel enters the Jewish mind as so great a rabbinic sage, a man beloved for his legal daring, passion for learning, remarkable openness to converts, and imaginative acts of kindness.

It is both in stories and in legal discussions that we encounter Hillel's willingness to define—in one extended sentence, no less—Judaism's essence, his openness to determining Jewish law not only on the basis of tradition but also on the basis of his keen understanding of the Torah's intention and his loving confidence in the instincts of the common man.†

But as familiar as Hillel's teachings are in the Jewish world

---

* See the glossary for an explanation of these terms. Because the schools of Hillel and Shammai so closely represent the views and personalities of their founders, their views and rulings are cited in later chapters in which Hillel and Shammai are compared and contrasted. As Adin Steinsaltz comments: "Even after more than a hundred years of disputes, during which the ideas changed and developed, the personalities of Shammai and Hillel were still the formative factors of each House" (Adin Steinsaltz, *Talmudic Images*, p. 17).

† It is also from these stories that I came to believe that Hillel might have responded quite differently to the young couple who came into my friend's office.

(and were repeatedly affirmed—by a heavenly voice, no less—as valid and fundamental), many of his most important ideas have been ignored, sometimes profoundly so. Who was this man whose teachings can feel as radical today as they must have been in his own time, and yet who sits, or ought to sit, squarely at the center of normative Judaism? And how have we moved so far from his vision? Understanding why this has happened—and why Hillel's vision must be reclaimed today—is what motivated me to write this book.

PART I

"While Standing on One Foot":
The Unique Teachings of Hillel

1

Hillel, the Most Ardent of Students

Rabbi Israel Meir Kagan (1838–1933), popularly known in Jewish life by the title of his first book, *Chafetz Chayyim*, founded and headed a yeshiva in the Belarus (White Russia) town of Radin. Students streamed to the yeshiva from throughout Europe. During World War I, a student from Germany was arrested by the czarist police and charged with spying for his native land. The defense lawyer asked the Chafetz Chayyim to appear in court as a character witness. Before summoning the rabbi to the witness stand, the lawyer, it is reported, approached the judge and said, "Your honor, the rabbi who is about to testify has an impeccable reputation among his fellow Jews. They tell a story that one day he came home and saw a thief rummaging through his living room. The frightened thief climbed out a window and ran off with some of the rabbi's possessions, and the rabbi ran after him, shouting, 'I declare all my property ownerless,' so that the thief would not be guilty of having committed a crime."

The judge looked at the lawyer skeptically. "Do you believe that story really happened?"

"I don't know, your honor," the lawyer answered, "but they don't tell stories like that about you and me."

The story with which Hillel enters Jewish consciousness presents him like an angel suspended above the heads of the two sages who were to become his greatest teachers. Nevertheless, it is an earthbound story that tells us that Hillel was poor, that he was hungry for learning, and that he knew what it was like to be, literally, an outsider looking in:

It was reported of Hillel the Elder that every day he used to work and earn one *tropaik*,* half of which he would give to the doorkeeper at the House of Learning; the other half he would spend for his and his family's food. One day he found no work, and the guard at the House of Learning would not permit him to enter. Hillel climbed [to the roof] and sat upon the skylight to hear the words of the living God from the mouths of [Rabbis]† Shmaya and Avtalion. That day was the eve of the Sabbath, during the winter, and snow fell upon him from heaven. When the dawn rose, Shmaya said to Avtalion, "Brother Avtalion, on every day this house is light and today it is dark. Is it perhaps a cloudy day?"

* A *tropaik* is half a dinar, not a large amount for a day's work.
† The word "rabbi" was not yet in use as a title for religious scholars (it was introduced during the mid-first century C.E., and was first used to describe Hillel's grandson, Rabbi Gamliel the Elder). I put the term here in brackets to underscore that these men were religious authorities, indeed the preeminent scholars and leaders of their time.

They looked up and saw the figure of a man on the sky-light. They climbed to the roof and found Hillel, covered by three *amot* (cubits) of snow. They removed him, bathed and anointed him, placed him opposite the fire, and said, "This man deserves to have the Sabbath laws violated on his behalf." (*Yoma* 35b)

There are a number of unusual, even odd, details in this story. For one thing, this is the first time we hear of a *Beit Midrash*, a center of learning, charging tuition to hear the teacher's lectures; it is particularly strange that payment is collected on a daily basis, like attendance at a theater.

In addition, while it does snow every few years in Jerusalem, it is an unusual coincidence that Hillel mounts the roof on precisely such an inclement day. But what strains credulity even more is the amount of snow that covers Hillel; three cubits, or about four and a half feet. Even with winds, it is unheard of for Jerusalem to develop such deep drifts. The fact that Hillel remains on the roof for many hours in the face of what must have been a raging storm seems intended to underscore that this is a man who is literally willing to risk his life to learn Torah.

It also introduces Hillel as a man whose nose is pressed to the glass of Jewish learning, the sort of man who might well identify with the seekers who later come to him seeking conversion.

Yet another odd detail: we hear nowhere else of a yeshiva being in session on Friday evening (the Sabbath eve), and then apparently remaining in session throughout the night and into the morning. The general tradition in Jewish life is that formal school study is adjourned before the Sabbath begins. Hillel, like all married men, would have been expected to be home for the Sabbath with his wife and family.

The fact that the school remains in session enables the story to communicate, in passing, an important lesson in Jewish law. Hillel's life is at risk by the time he is brought down from the roof into the study hall. There, a fire is carefully tended so that it will gradually warm him, and acts involving maintaining the fire—behavior that would normally be prohibited on the Sabbath—are performed on his behalf.

The two scholars heading the yeshiva, Shmaya and Avtalion, approve of doing all that is necessary to save Hillel, since "this man deserves that the Shabbat be violated on his behalf."

This statement is puzzling because Jewish law requires the violation of Shabbat whenever life is in danger. Nowhere in Jewish legal writings is it recorded that one has to practice the extraordinary virtues of a Hillel to be entitled to have the Sabbath violated on his or her behalf.

Yet, Shmaya and Avtalion's statement suggests a possibly different reality, that perhaps violating the Sabbath to save a life was not yet regarded as definitely permitted in Jewish law. Maybe the Sabbath, at least in some minds, superseded in sanctity the value of human life.

We know that there were in earlier times Jews who adhered to such a belief. Approximately a century before this incident with Hillel, Jewish life had been rocked by the Maccabean revolt against the Hellenist government of Antiochus Epiphanes, the Syrian monarch. The successful revolt, initiated by Mattathias and spearheaded by his son, Judah Maccabee, is commemorated to this day in the holiday of Hanukkah. Early on, at the revolt's inception, there was a group of Jews known as Hasidim (pious ones), who encountered Hellenist troops and fought against them. They continued to do so until the Sabbath, when the Hasidim dropped their weapons and allowed themselves to be annihilated by Antiochus's soldiers. At the time, Mattathias ruled with admirable common sense: "If we all do as our brothers have done . . . then [the Syrians] will soon wipe us off the face of the earth." The book of Maccabees records that on that day, the Jewish revolutionaries "decided that, if anyone came to fight against them on the Sabbath they would fight back, rather than all die as their brothers . . . had done" (1 Macc. 2:32–41).

So there was a precedent for engaging in forbidden activities on Shabbat when life was endangered, but perhaps there were still those who questioned a blanket permission to violate the Sabbath to save a life. What Shmaya and Avtalion asserted now, in unequivocal terms, is that for a person such as Hillel the Sabbath laws should be suspended.

Although there are elements in this story that have a legendary cast to them, certain definite details about Hillel are still communicated. First, we learn of his extraordinary devotion to Torah study, a commitment that has characterized Judaism's great religious teachers ever since[1] (it was said of the eighteenth-century Lithuanian rabbinic scholar, the Gaon of Vilna, that he studied Torah* eighteen to twenty hours a day). Hillel, though, is the first to personify this trait. As such, he created the paradigm. Second, the story communicates that Hillel is a poor man with an iron will. The fact that he is a day laborer with no spare money, yet rises to become the greatest rabbi of his age, conveys the message that the Talmud doesn't judge people on the basis of their wealth or societal status, but on the basis of their achievements.

Finally, the story exemplifies a principle Hillel would famously espouse: that acts of loving-kindness are what you begin with. Whatever the two Rabbis were teaching that day certainly mattered—it was their wisdom, after all, that kept Hillel there during a raging snowstorm. But even more significant was their behavior after class was over. Their actions—carrying a poor man down from the roof, tending to a fire on Shabbat, and recognizing, despite his poverty, Hillel's worthiness of character and worthiness to be a student—are what have conveyed ever since that moral behavior trumps social distinctions and sometimes even determines how Jewish law is to be decided. The rest is commentary.

* The term "Torah" as used in Jewish life refers not only to the first five books of the Bible, but is also a descriptive term that encompasses all sacred Jewish texts.

2

Hillel's Rise to Leadership

We know nothing of Hillel's life for many years after this event, much as if we learned of a poor student who, after a struggle, is admitted to Harvard and of whom we next hear many years later when he is appointed university president. In a sense, this is what happens now to Hillel.

While it is true that we know no details of Hillel's life during these years, we do know something about the historical circumstances then prevailing in Judea, circumstances that affected Hillel's promotion to a position of leadership. The most significant event was the rise to power of Herod, a vicious, though politically successful, monarch.

Herod's kingship over Israel was the indirect result of a terrible wrong committed some seventy years earlier by the Hasmonean king, John Hyrcanus. Hyrcanus made a decision to augment the Jewish population of Palestine by forcibly converting to Judaism one of the peoples he ruled, the Idumeans, who occupied a small state south of Jerusalem.*

---

* This is the only known instance of forced conversion by Jews in power. The Idumeans presumably were descendants of the biblical nation of Edom.

Here is another form of conversion many Jews do not often contemplate and that is, in fact, unusual, even unprecedented, in the annals of Jewish history. It may even be that this event lies behind at least some of the anxieties stirred up by the stories of conversion involving Hillel—the fear that the conversion of any Gentiles, forcible or peaceful, is a perilous undertaking. Among those brought to Judaism by this forced conversion was Antipas, whom the Hasmoneans appointed to serve as governor of Idumea. Herod was his grandson.[1]

Herod took control of Jerusalem in 37 B.C.E., with the support of the Roman army. A vile person, Herod inaugurated his regime by murdering forty-five members of the Sanhedrin (the combined legislature and high court of Jewish law). Realizing that most Judeans felt a greater loyalty to the Hasmoneans than to him, Herod was obsessed with removing all vestiges of Hasmonean rule. He took the high priesthood out of Hasmonean hands and assigned this most important spiritual office to men whose primary qualification was loyalty to him (regarding the low level of some of these High Priests, see p. 36). After disempowering the Sanhedrin, Herod established his own council, thereby ensuring that no one with ties to the Hasmoneans and no religious figure who questioned the validity of his family's forced conversion was a member. Herod was a Jewish nightmare, an insecure, tenuous Jew often in league with the enemies of Israel, and a violent reminder not merely of the consequences of forcible conversions, but perhaps to some of the consequences of Gentile conversion itself.

Herod did not fall into the category of people who are cruel only to outsiders but nice to their own family. He had his wife, the Hasmonean princess Mariamne, executed on charges of plotting to murder him (Herod had likely hoped that this marriage would gain him acceptance by Jews loyal to the Hasmoneans); after her execution, he appears to have regretted his behavior. Later, he charged his two sons from his marriage to Mariamne with conspiring to overthrow him—which they well might have, given that he had murdered their mother—and executed them as well, thereby ensuring the elimination of potential heirs with "Hasmonean blood." A few days before his death, Herod had yet another son, Antipater, from a different marriage, executed on the same charge, leading the Roman emperor Augustus to comment, "It would be better to be Herod's swine than his son." For good measure, he also murdered his mother-in-law and arranged to have his brother-in-law, the High Priest, drowned.

Herod tried to win over the Jewish population with an enormous and beautiful expansion of the Temple in Jerusalem, an effort that occupied ten thousand laborers and a thousand priests for nine years. But he also built an idolatrous temple in Shomron and turned Caesarea into a pagan city. He built a circus there, where, in addition to foot and chariot races, he presented gladiator fights and battles between human beings and wild animals. Ironically, it was this lackey of Rome who rebuilt Masada, which a century later served as the final outpost of the Jewish revolt against Rome.

We can only speculate on what Hillel was doing during Herod's early years in power. It is possible that he returned for some years to Babylon, his native land (we have very little knowledge about Babylonian-Jewish life at this time). Or perhaps, as one Jewish scholar conjectured, he went to live in the Judean desert among the ascetic Dead Sea Sects.[2] Alternatively, he may have remained in the area of Jerusalem and led a quiet, contemplative life of study during this time of persecution. This experience might have been behind his otherwise enigmatic epigram, "If you see a generation to which the Torah is dear [that is, appreciated], spread it . . . but if you see a generation to which the Torah is not dear, gather it and keep it to yourself" (*Berakhot* 63a).

What is striking is that Herod's kingship (37–4 B.C.E.) overlaps for more than a quarter of a century with Hillel's years of leadership (c. 30 B.C.E.–10 C.E.). But we find no stories—even apocryphal ones—recording contact between the two men.

During Herod's early years, he apparently appointed the Bnai Beteira as the country's new religious leaders. We know little about these men, though it seems that they (or their families), like Hillel, came from Babylon. Herod favored assigning high offices to Jews from the Diaspora, people whose loyalty would be to him and not to the deposed Hasmoneans.

The Bnai Beteira had their virtues (most notably, as we shall see, humility), but in-depth religious scholarship was not one of them. It is clear that they had not studied, and had no relationship, with Shmaya and Avtalion. An important question arose some time around 30 B.C.E. Passover was approaching and was due that year to begin on a Friday night. Today, of course, the primary association Jews have with the first night of Passover is the Seder. To this day, on the Seder plate, Jews place a shank bone, commemorating the paschal lamb that their ancestors brought to sacrifice in Jerusalem during the time the Temple stood. For Jews living during the time of the Temple, the bringing of the sacrifice was as important an association with the holiday as was the Seder meal that followed it. Jews would come to Jerusalem from throughout the country, and even from abroad, to sacrifice a lamb, and the family would eat the lamb while conducting the Seder meal.

The Passover sacrifice was so central a ritual that the Torah decreed *karet*, the cutting off from the Israelite people, for anyone who did not bring the Passover sacrifice at its appointed time (see Num. 9:13). And that is exactly what the source of the Bnai Beteira's dilemma was. On the one hand, not bringing the sacrifice at the right time was unthinkable. On the other hand, slaughtering and preparing an animal involves activities that are normally forbidden on the Sabbath. Two of Judaism's most important rituals, the Passover sacrifice and the Sabbath (the only ritual law specified in the Ten Commandments), were at odds, and the highly conflicted Bnai Beteira couldn't decide which took precedence.[3] The Talmud conveys the sense of anxiety and increasing panic that must have prevailed with Passover rapidly approaching, tens of thousands of Jews preparing to come to

Jerusalem, and the religious leadership not knowing what to do:

> On one occasion, the fourteenth of Nisan [the day on which Passover begins] fell on the Sabbath. The Bnai Beteira forgot the law and did not know whether or not slaughter of the Passover sacrifice overrode the Sabbath restrictions. They said, "Is there no man who knows whether or not the Passover sacrifice overrides the Sabbath?" They were told, "There is a man who came here from Babylon, and his name is Hillel the Babylonian. He served the two great men of the generation, Shmaya and Avtalion, and he will know whether or not the Passover sacrifice overrides the Sabbath." They sent for him, and said, "Do you then know whether or not the Passover sacrifice overrides the Sabbath?" (*Pesachim* 66a)

Hillel was well aware of what Shmaya and Avtalion ruled in such a case, but he did not share the answer right away. He wished to use logical arguments to show the Bnai Beteira the correct way to act. Given the choice between relying on tradition (citing the ruling of Shmaya and Avtalion) or on principles of logic, Hillel's instinct was to favor logic.[4] He therefore responded with a rhetorical question: "But is there then only a single Passover sacrifice during the year that overrides the Sabbath? Are there not more than two hundred 'Passover sacrifices' during the year that override the Sabbath?" What Hillel was alluding to was the fact that throughout the year priests bring certain communal sacrifices on the Sabbath. For rhetorical purposes, Hillel referred to these offerings as "Passover sacrifices," but what he really meant was that there are two hundred instances throughout the year in which Sabbath prohibitions are overridden in order to offer a sacrifice. For example, the *Mussaf* sacrifice is brought on Shabbat. Hillel argued that if the *Mussaf* sacrifice overrides the Sabbath, then certainly the Passover sacrifice, whose nonperformance is punished by being cut off from the Jewish people, obviously should do so.

In one version of this episode, the Bnai Beteira are convinced by this argument, and "immediately seat him at the head and appoint him as *nasi* (leader, or prince) over them" (*Pesachim* 66a). In another, however, the Bnai Beteira refuse to accept Hillel's arguments and try to refute his logic. At one point, they even insult him, saying, "We have already said, 'Is there something good that can come from the Babylonian?' . . . Even though Hillel sat and expounded to them all day long, they did not accept the teaching from him until he told them [using the language of an oath], 'May evil befall me [if I am lying]. Thus I have heard from Shmaya and Avtalion [that the Passover sacrifice overrides the Sabbath]' " (Jerusalem Talmud, *Pesachim* 6:1). According to this version of the episode, at that point the Bnai Beteira appoint him as leader.

Whichever version one accepts, this story is central, for from this point on Hillel becomes the leading religious teacher of his generation, a position he holds for some forty years. Yet the Talmud tells us of an uncharacteristic event that happens within hours of Hillel's appointment, one of

only two instances in the dozens of stories told about Hillel
in which he speaks sharply, even a bit unpleasantly.* At one
point in the discussion with the Bnai Beteira, he turns to
them and says, "What caused this to occur to you, that I
should come up from Babylon and become the leader over
you? It was the laziness (*atzilut*) that was in you, that you
did not bother to serve the two great ones of the generation,
Shmaya and Avtalion."⁵

This was, of course, a rather sharp, even mean-spirited,
way to speak, particularly in public. The Talmud records
that Hillel is immediately punished for his words. A question is posed to him: "What is the law if a person forgot and
did not bring a knife [for sacrificing animals] to the Temple
with him before the Sabbath?" What should the person do,
since transporting a knife is not something one can do on the
Sabbath? The suddenly abashed Hillel has to acknowledge,
"I heard this law once, but I have forgotten it," but he then
goes on to say, "However, leave it to the people. If they are
not themselves prophets, they are the children of prophets
[and will know what to do]." The next day, the following
occurred: "One whose Passover offering was a sheep stuck
the knife into the animal's wool [so that the sheep carried
the knife to the Temple]. And one whose Passover offering

---

* In both instances, Hillel seems to have been provoked by derogatory references made to his being a Babylonian. In the other instance he asked some
men who were carrying wheat how much they charged for their work, and
when he questioned their high price, they called him a "stupid Babylonian,"
whereupon he called them "wretched fools." Nonetheless, the text indicates that he then spent time with the men and reconciled (*The Fathers
According to Rabbi Nathan*, chap. 12).

was a goat stuck the knife between its horns and had the goat carry it to the Temple." Hillel, observing these actions, remembered the law and said, "I received this very teaching from the mouths of Shmaya and Avtalion" (*Pesachim* 66a).[6]

A new leader had now arisen in Israel, a man whose knowledge of the tradition was unparalleled, but who was willing to supplement the tradition with lessons derived from logic and with an awareness of and respect for the behavior of the people around him. This amalgamation of tradition, logic, and appreciation for the common man drew Hillel to new types of conclusions, some of which, as we shall see, still have the capacity, two thousand years later, to lead the Jewish people in new, potentially world-transforming, directions.

3

"While Standing on One Foot"

Hillel's willingness to run the risk of freezing to death is the story with which he enters Jewish consciousness. The story in which he defines Judaism's essence to a non-Jewish questioner is the story that has kept him there ever since. It is the Talmud's most famous story and one also known—unlike almost any other story in the Talmud—to many Christians:

> There was [an] incident involving a Gentile who came before Shammai and said to him: "Convert me to Judaism on condition that you will teach me the entire Torah while I stand on one foot." Shammai pushed the man away with the building rod he was holding. Undeterred, the man then came before Hillel with the same request. Hillel said to him, "That which is hateful unto you, do not do unto your neighbor. This is the whole Torah, all the rest is commentary. Now, go and study." (*Shabbat* 31a)

Well-known as this story is, I find that it is generally related with one detail changed. The change occurs in how people usually begin the story: "A non-Jew asked Hillel to define Judaism's essence while he [the non-Jew] was standing on one foot." If that had been the non-Jew's request, Hillel's response would have been less surprising. People who present their religious teachings to outsiders often focus on their religion's more humanistic and universalistic elements. But what the non-Jew asked of Hillel was more in the nature of a legal request, one requiring a legal response. He asked to be *converted* to Judaism on condition that Hillel define for him Judaism's essence. In that context, what is striking is that Hillel does not speak to the man about belief in God or about the importance of observing the Sabbath and Jewish holidays, even though belief in God is Judaism's core belief and the observance of Judaism's ritual laws was one of Hillel's central concerns.* He was, of course, a fully observant Jew. Nonetheless, when asked what is most basic for a non-Jew to know before he can convert, Hillel restricts himself to a description of Judaism's ethical essence and then adds, "This is the whole Torah! All the rest is commentary! Now, go and study."

The fact that Hillel is willing to offer so brief an explanation—fifteen words in the popularly spoken Aramaic—indicates that there is a central focus to his understanding of Judaism, one that provides him with a standard that later enables him to modify certain Torah laws

---

* If you examine the legal discussions in which Hillel is cited in the Mishnah, the Tosefta, and the Talmud, the primary focus is on ritual issues (see, for example, footnote 1 on p. 229).

in a manner that will shock other rabbis. Only if one understands Judaism as having an ethical essence can one conclude, as Hillel did on several occasions, that sometimes practicing the Torah *literally* can lead one to violate the Torah's ethical will (for examples of this, see chapter 5).

Regarding the unusual question posed by the non-Jew, Talmud scholar Edward Gershfield speculates that the request was characteristic

> of the Hellenistic intellectual. Many of the philosophical schools of the time strove to give clear and concise statements of their views. For some, especially the Stoics, clarity and simplicity were in themselves evidence of truth. Thus, as Hillel perceived, this speaker was speaking out of the context of the Gentile intellectual world. He was implying that if the Torah had something to say, it could be stated simply and clearly, and, if so, he wanted to hear it. If the message of the Torah could be understood only after much long-winded explanation, that in itself would argue against it being valid.[1]

Hillel's response is in effect a negative formulation of the Torah's most famous commandment, "Love your neighbor as yourself." But why did Hillel not simply quote the Torah verse, which, in its evocation of "love," certainly has a more upbeat quality to it? Why did he resort to a negative formulation?

Here we're in the realm of conjecture. I suspect that Hillel wanted to offer his questioner a principle he could incorporate into his life immediately. "Love your neighbor as yourself," if understood literally, makes demands of us that are sometimes unclear and that few of us are ready to satisfy. For example, does this law obligate you to share all your belongings with others? Maybe yes (the verse would seem to suggest that), maybe no (which is what I suspect most of us feel), but to declare this commandment without extensive explanation could easily confuse the listener. Similarly, you could argue that this verse would oblige us to mourn the death of an acquaintance with the same intensity with which we would mourn the death of a member of our immediate family. After all, if we are commanded to love others as we love ourselves, why wouldn't we be commanded to mourn the loss of others as we would mourn the loss of those dearest to us?[2]

Hillel's negative formulation, on the other hand, is much easier to incorporate into daily behavior. Before engaging in an act, we should ask ourselves, "How would I feel if that person treated me in the manner I am now preparing to treat him?" Or, "How would I feel if that person spoke about me in the manner I am now speaking about her?" Posing these questions to ourselves is within everyone's capacity and, if our determination is strong, the answers yielded are not difficult to incorporate into our behavior.

My friend Dr. Isaac Herschkopf, a psychiatrist, argues: "Hillel may have been emulating God's articulation of the Ten Commandments. Thus, God did not command us to be honest, truthful, and faithful. Rather, He commanded us, 'Don't steal,' 'Don't bear false witness,' 'Don't commit adultery.' It may be less positive, but it is undeniably more effective."

That Hillel was willing to convert the man to Judaism upon his acceptance of this principle shows that Hillel's belief in ethics as Judaism's central teaching was not rhetoric. He meant it.

What he also meant with equal passion—and this part of his message is often ignored—are his final words to the man, "Now, go and study." Without study and a knowledge of Jewish holy texts, Judaism becomes literally contentless (the question "What does Judaism want me to do?" becomes unanswerable). That is why Hillel is so insistent on the importance of ongoing study. I often meet Jews who are passionately political, and given the political orientation of most American Jews, that means they are usually liberal, though a fervent minority are conservative. I ask such people if they ever find themselves studying Jewish texts that challenge their liberalism or conservatism. If they don't— and few of them I find do—that means, in effect, that their real religion is liberalism or conservatism, with a smattering of biblical and Talmudic quotes cited to support whatever position they already believe.*

Zil g'mar, "Go and study," are Hillel's final words to the new convert and, in essence, to each of us. With the proper amount of study, when you try to decide how to behave, you will have more than good intentions upon which to rely, you

---

* In contrast, as Rabbi Irwin Kula notes, the Talmud records that Hillel's disciples assiduously studied views with which they disagreed (see p. 120).

will have a three-thousand-year-old body of teachings, arguments, and discussions from which to draw (for examples of such wisdom, see chapters 13–17). If you are willing to accept Hillel's ethical summary statement and devote yourself to ongoing study, then, indeed, all the rest will be commentary.

Not a small amount of wisdom to communicate in fifteen words.

4

Hillel and the Three Converts

On the Bible and Conversion

The common perception that Judaism has no interest in non-Jews becoming Jewish is reinforced by the equally common perception that the Torah knows nothing of conversion to the Israelite religion. Both perceptions are wrong. Already in the time of the Torah there existed a mechanism by which foreigners could join the community: "You shall not abhor an Edomite for he is your kinsman.* You shall not abhor an Egyptian for you were a stranger in his land. Children born to them may be admitted into the congregation of the Lord in the third generation" (Deut. 23:8–9). This ruling presumably meant that after living among the Israelites for

---

* The Edomites were the descendants of Esau, the patriarch Jacob's brother, and hence regarded as distant kinsmen of Israel. Another statement in Deuteronomy (23:4) forbidding Ammonites and Moabites from entering "the congregation of the Lord" likewise implies that members of other groups could join the Israelite community (see Louis Feldman, *Jew and Gentile in the Ancient World*, p. 288). As noted (see p. 9), a millennium after this biblical ruling, the Edomites were forcibly converted to Judaism by the Hasmonean king, John Hyrcanus.

two generations, the grandchildren of Edomites and Egyptians could be admitted into the community.*

Later biblical books express an explicit desire for Jews to spread their teachings beyond the Jewish world. The prophet Isaiah (seventh century B.C.E.) foresees the day when non-Jews will say: "Come, let us go up to the Mount of the Lord, the House of the God of Jacob [i.e., the Temple in Jerusalem], that He may instruct us in His ways, and that we may walk in His paths. For Torah shall come forth from Zion, and the word of the Lord from Jerusalem" (Isa. 2:3–4). In Isaiah's penultimate verse (Isa. 66:23), he speaks of a time when people throughout the world will observe the Sabbath and worship God.

The short biblical book of Ruth introduces for the first time a vivid description of a non-Hebrew accepting the Israelite religion and becoming a part of its people. Ruth, a Moabite, marries a man named Machlon who, during a famine, had left Israel with his parents and brother to live in the nearby nation of Moab. After Machlon's early death, Ruth makes the decision to accompany her mother-in-law, Naomi, who has decided to return to Israel. Naomi repeatedly encourages Ruth to go back to her family (apparently, she is still a young woman who can marry again and start her life anew), but Ruth refuses to. Rather, she tells Naomi:

---

*In the Gutnick edition of the Bible, a Torah translation and commentary published by the Lubavitch movement, the presumption of conversion is incorporated into the translation of verse 9: "Children who are born to them, in the third generation may (convert and marry a Jewish woman) and enter the congregation of God" (p. 1277).

"Your people shall be my people, your God shall be my God" (Ruth 1:16). "Your people shall be my people"—in other words, "I want to become part of the Israelite people"; "Your God shall be my God"—in other words, "I want to accept the Israelite religion." Three thousand years after she spoke these words, this inseparable fusion of peoplehood and religion continues to distinguish Judaism from other faiths.

Ruth goes to Israel with Naomi and eventually marries Boaz, her late husband's cousin. They have a son, Oved, whom the Bible records as the grandfather of King David (Ruth 4:21–22).[1] Since the Jewish tradition teaches that the Messiah will descend from David, it follows that the Messiah will also be a direct descendant of Ruth. What a testament to Judaism's high regard for people who join the Jewish community.[2] And since the Talmud records that Hillel is a descendant of David (Jerusalem Talmud, *Ta'anit* 4:2), it follows that Hillel, too, traces his ancestry to Ruth, the Moabite woman who joined the Jewish people.

Today, when we hear of a non-Jew inquiring about becoming Jewish, we often assume that the non-Jew has forged a romantic connection with a Jew, and has perhaps been told that he or she must convert if a marriage is to take place. Alternatively, there are non-Jews whose initial motives for converting are from the beginning a direct response to Judaism. Such people may have been attracted through something they read, a lecture they heard, or perhaps through exposure to religiously committed Jews. Not infrequently, rabbis are approached today by non-Jews who have learned of a Jewish ancestor and are now interested in looking into their forebear's religion.

The notion of non-Jews seeking out Judaism is not new.[3] While there is not a great deal of material about converts in the Talmud, the rabbi who figures most prominently in the stories that are told about proselytes is Hillel; he appears in three such incidents. In all three, the non-Jews first approach Hillel's contemporary, Shammai, from whom they receive a negative, hostile response. In the story cited in the previous chapter, Shammai lifts up a measuring rod he is holding (he is a builder) and drives the man off. Although this behavior was the height of incivility, I have some measure of sympathy for Shammai's annoyance. Every writer knows what it means to be asked to condense into a single sentence a book he has worked on for years. How much worse to be pressed to distill the essence of an ancient tradition whose very essence may be that it has no essence but lives inside a complex, endlessly ramifying system of law and ritual, and that does not lend itself—at least in Shammai's view—to a brief and highly condensed mission statement.[4]

It is of course to this very non-Jew that Hillel simply replies: "What is hateful unto you, do not do unto your neighbor. This is the whole Torah, all the rest is commentary. Now, go and study." The non-Jew seems to accept this definition, and Hillel converts him. Does Hillel first spend months studying Jewish texts and laws with the man? If he does, the Talmud does not record this. Does Hillel first arrange to have a learned student brief the non-Jew on every detail of the laws of Sabbath observance and the dietary laws that comprise kashrut (two areas that remain the primary, but by no means exclusive, components of a religiously observant Jewish life)? Again, the Talmud does not tell us. What we are told is that he converts the man.*

Had this been the only instance of a non-Jew approaching Hillel for conversion, we might conclude that Hillel saw the ethical principle as so central a component of Judaism that he deemed any non-Jew who accepted this principle as worthy of immediate acceptance into the Jewish people.

But when we turn to the stories of the other two non-Jews who come to Hillel with requests for conversion, we see that they suggest very different conditions for becoming Jewish, ones that do not relate to any specific ethical principle, and that Hillel converts them speedily as well. We therefore learn something important. Hillel is so open to non-Jews becoming Jewish that when someone approaches him with an interest in Judaism, his inclination is to convert the person, or certainly to ease and speed the process for doing so.

In one of these stories, the non-Jew has the equal misfor-

---

* The two ritual acts Jewish law demands of converts are circumcision in the case of males, and immersion in a *mikvah*, a ritual bath, in the case of both males and females. The Talmud does not record Hillel's performance of these rituals, but given the centrality of these acts (Abraham enters the covenant with God by circumcision at the age of ninety-nine and God instructs that all his descendants must be circumcised; see Gen. 17:9–27), their performance can be assumed. A Talmudic commentary assumes that Hillel was certain the man would become fully observant.

tune of first approaching Shammai. The man sets before Shammai an extremely irritating condition. In the words of the Talmud: "It once happened that a non-Jew came before Shammai and asked him: 'How many Torahs do you Jews have?' Shammai replied, 'Two, the Written Torah and the Oral Torah [the rabbinic explanations of how Torah laws are practiced]. The non-Jew then said to him, 'As for the Written Torah, I believe you, but concerning the Oral Torah, I don't believe you [that it is the will of God, and therefore binding]. Convert me to Judaism on condition that you teach me only the Written Torah'" (*Shabbat* 31a). Shammai rebukes the man for his insolence and sends him on his way with an insult. A short time later, the man comes before Hillel, makes the same request, and Hillel converts him. Hillel then immediately sets about teaching the man the Hebrew alphabet, "Aleph, Bet, Gimmel, Daled," and so on. The following day, Hillel reverses the names of the letters (calling an Aleph a Bet, for example) and the man protests, "But yesterday, didn't you tell me the opposite?" Hillel replies: "If you rely upon me to recognize the letters of the alphabet, then rely on me also about the truth of the Oral Law." In other words, if you're depending on me to teach you the Torah, rely on me when I explain to you how the Torah is to be understood, and what constitutes Torah.

A few comments about this story: The Written Torah refers to the first five books of the Hebrew Bible, the books that are often called in English the Pentateuch.* Genesis, the

---

* Genesis, Exodus, Leviticus, Numbers, and Deuteronomy.

first of these books, contains the stories of Adam and Eve; Abraham, Isaac, Jacob, and Joseph; and Sarah, Rebecca, Rachel, and Leah. The final four books tell of Moses, the story of the Exodus, God's revelation at Sinai and the Ten Commandments, and the forty years of wandering in the desert. Along the way, the Torah reveals what tradition numbers as 613 commandments, the basis of all Jewish law. But alongside these written commandments, Judaism possesses an Oral Law (originally unwritten but later recorded in the Talmud). Traditional Jewish teachings—associated with the Second Temple–era sect known as the Pharisees—hold that many of these laws, explanations of how the Torah laws are to be fulfilled, date back to the revelation at Sinai. In other words, along with the written Torah, Moses was also instructed in an Oral Law. That some sort of Oral Law has existed from Judaism's earliest times is self-evident, since the Torah cannot serve as a self-sufficient document. For example, in the opening paragraph of the Shema, the Israelites are instructed to "tie them as a sign upon your hand, and put them as *totafot* between your eyes." The passage might be easy to understand if we had clear knowledge of what *totafot* are. But we don't. The word is used several times in the Bible, but always in the same context, speaking of putting *totafot* between your eyes.

The Oral Law explains that the word refers to tefillin, the phylacteries that Jewish men are supposed to don weekday mornings, placing one on the foreheads between the eyes, and the other on one arm ("a sign upon your hand").[5] In short, some sort of Oral Law has always been necessary to explain passages in the Bible that would otherwise be inexplicable. For example, in Deuteronomy 12:21, Moses, speaking in God's Name, tells the Israelites that if they wish to eat meat, "you may slaughter any of the cattle or sheep that the Lord gives you, as I have instructed you." But we look in vain for any verses in the Torah with instructions about how to carry out the kosher slaughter of animals. Clearly, Moses is referring here to some sort of supplementary Oral Law through which these laws and procedures were transmitted.

The Oral Law is necessary for other reasons as well. While 613 commandments might sound like a lot,[6] they are hardly sufficient to cover every exigency in a person's or a nation's life. For example, the Torah takes marriage for granted. Early in Genesis, when God creates Eve as a companion to Adam, the Bible makes it clear that marriage should be the natural state for human beings: "Therefore shall a man leave his father and mother and cleave to his wife and they shall be one flesh" (Gen. 2:24). Later, the Bible describes the wedding of Jacob to Leah (unfortunately for Jacob, he thinks he is marrying Rachel). Other marriages also are recorded in the Bible. But nowhere does the Bible record how an actual wedding ceremony is conducted, or any words that need to be said or documents that need to be signed. Rather, the marriage ceremony, eventually set down by the rabbis, is part of the Oral Law.

Therefore, when the non-Jew says to Shammai, "I am willing to accept the Written Torah but not the Oral Torah," he is, in essence, saying, "I want to become a Jew, but a totally different kind of Jew than you and all the other Jews. I want to become a Jew on my terms, not yours, but still I insist that you convert me." To revert to a modern-day analogy, it would be as if a man were to come before a judge to be confirmed as an American citizen. But then, just before the swearing in takes place, he tells the judge that he willingly accepts as binding all the laws of the Constitution, but not the rulings of the Supreme Court concerning how the Constitution is to be understood and applied.

Would the judge accept such a condition? No—and neither would Shammai.

But Hillel, as we have seen, regards this more as a teaching opportunity and is in no way disheartened or antagonized by the man's demand.

The third non-Jew who wishes to be converted gives the initial impression of being a bit simpleminded. The Talmud describes him as walking past a Jewish school where he hears a teacher expounding on a verse from the Torah dealing with some special clothing: "These are the vestments they are to make: a breastpiece, an ephod, a robe, a fringed tunic, a headdress, and a sash." (Exod. 28:4). The man is intrigued by what sounds like some very elaborate and ornate garments and inquires, "For whom are these lavish garments?" He is told that it is for the High Priest. The man reasons to himself—this is the basis for my assuming him to be simple—"I will go and convert to Judaism so that they will appoint me High Priest."

He goes to Shammai and announces, "Convert me to Judaism on condition that you have me appointed High Priest."

Imagine Shammai's mind-set at this point. It's not enough that a non-Jew asks him to reduce a lifetime of study to a few phrases, or that another non-Jew asks him, in effect, to reject the very teachings that define Pharisaic Judaism, the cause to which he has devoted his life. Now, a Gentile is demanding to be converted so that he can be immediately appointed to the highest spiritual position in Jewish life. It is, after all, the High Priest who enters the Holy of Holies in the Temple in Jerusalem on Yom Kippur to offer prayers on the nation's behalf before God. Clearly, Shammai regards the man as a nuisance at best, or as exceedingly arrogant at worst, and again raises the measuring rod in his hand (perhaps just a long ruler) and chases the man away.

Undeterred, the man goes to Hillel and poses the same request: "Convert me to Judaism on condition that you have me appointed as High Priest." Hillel converts him.

Why? The text gives no indication of what motivates Hillel to do so; the man does, after all, seem to be a somewhat unworthy candidate. But then, master pedagogue that he is, Hillel makes a commonsense request of the man: "Can we appoint anyone as king unless he is familiar with the ceremonies of royalty? Go and learn about the ceremonies of royalty [in this case, the regulations applying to the priesthood]." The man starts to study the relevant biblical passages and soon comes across the verse, "You shall make Aaron and his sons [and descendants] responsible for observing their priestly duties, and any stranger [that is, a non-priest] who approaches [to perform the duties of the priest] shall die" (Num. 3:10; see also 18:7).

The man asks Hillel, "About whom is this verse stated?" Hillel answers, "It is said even about David, king of Israel."

The man reasons to himself, "If it says concerning native-born Israelites who are not of priestly descent, 'the stranger who approaches shall die,' how much more will *I* be regarded as a stranger?"

From this story alone, we witness Hillel's ability to model the most effective form of teaching, one that leads the student himself to the appropriate conclusion without forcing it upon him.

And now, for just a moment, the Talmud shifts gears and lets this new convert assume center stage. There is a biblical commandment: "Do not hate your brother in your heart," which is understood in Jewish law as meaning that if somebody has hurt you, you should not keep the animosity bottled up inside, but express the hurt to the person who inflicted it and, if necessary, criticize the person: "Reprove, yes, reprove your fellow" (Lev. 19:17). So the man heads straight back to Shammai and says to him, "Could I possibly have been fit to be High Priest? Is it not written in the Torah, 'A stranger who comes near shall die'?"

The Talmud quotes no more of what the man says, but it is clear what he is conveying to the quick-tempered Shammai: Why did you treat me like a creature with whom you don't bother to reason and whom you chase away with a stick? You could have explained to me, even in a sentence or two, the laws of priesthood and why I was not qualified to be a priest.

The Talmud does not record any response by Shammai to

the man's disapproval, but this tale is clearly written in a manner sympathetic to the convert. It is also interesting that in *Ethics of the Fathers*, Shammai is credited with the teaching, "Receive every man with a cheerful expression" (*Pirkei Avot* 1:15). Who knows? Perhaps this teaching was formulated in the aftermath of this man's criticism.

The convert, aware now of just how audacious his earlier request to Hillel had been, seeks out Hillel and says to him: "Let blessings come to rest upon your head, for through your guidance you brought me under the wings of the Divine Presence."

The stories of Hillel and the three converts challenge three common and widely held assumptions of Jewish life: that Judaism is not interested in non-Jews converting; that if a non-Jew comes to convert, the rabbi's first obligation is to discourage him from doing so; and that a conversion should be valid only if the proselyte formally undertakes to fully observe all Jewish laws.* There is certainly a basis for these

* The late Rabbi Immanuel Jakobovits (chief rabbi of England), basing himself on a teaching in the Talmud—"If a heathen is prepared to accept the Torah except for one law, we must not receive him"—*Bekhorot* 30b—explained why a candidate who makes so provocative a statement should be rejected:

> I believe . . . in laying down the basic condition that we want [converts] to accept the totality of Jewish law, just as I am expected to accept the totality of the constitution of the United States. If I say that I will not accept that totality, that I will make an exception, I will be rejected as [a candidate to become] an American citizen. If anyone comes to me and says that he cannot accept the totality of Jewish law—the Jewish constitution of life—then I must say, for precisely the same reason, that I cannot assume the responsibility for converting him.

attitudes in the Talmud (see, for example, *Kiddushin* 70b, *Yevamot* 47a, and the note below), but it is also clear that these teachings are not the whole story.

In light of the behavior of a rabbi such as Shammai, what is remarkable is just how open Hillel is to converts. Perhaps this is in part because, as the Talmud mentions, Hillel's two most significant teachers, Shmaya and Avtalion, were descended from converts (*Gittin* 57b). Presumably, Shmaya and Avtalion were Shammai's teachers as well, and so that explanation, like many others, may dissolve before the mystery of temperament and character. Perhaps Hillel was simply someone who was open to others, whether through inborn disposition or hard-earned experience, and he saw that openness as a natural part of Judaism's mission.

This is not to discount the effect on Hillel of his teachers' backgrounds. He might well have been sympathetic to would-be converts because he understood from personal experience that converts and their descendants could turn into wonderful Jews. He also understood that there were people who had been cruel to Shmaya and Avtalion specifically because of their backgrounds. The Talmud relates: "There was an incident involving a certain High Priest who came out of the Temple on Yom Kippur after performing the service. And all the people were following him home in a display of respect. But as soon as they saw Shmaya and Avtal-

---

(See Immanuel Jakobovits and David Max Eichhorn, "Shall Jews Missionize?" pp. 146–47). The article, a record of a debate between the Orthodox Jakobovits and the Reform Eichhorn, is reprinted in Lawrence Epstein, *Readings on Conversion to Judaism*.

ion, they left the High Priest and followed Shmaya and Avtalion instead. After a while, the two rabbis came to take leave of the High Priest, and he greeted them scornfully: 'May the descendants of Gentiles go in peace.' " Hillel, surely aware of such stories, might well have decided to compensate with the greatest kindness for the elitist behavior displayed by some to would-be converts, to converts, and to their descendants. It should also be noted that Hillel's teachers gave as good as they got. Shmaya and Avtalion retorted: 'May the descendants of Gentiles who do the work of Aaron [Israel's original High Priest] go in peace, but may the descendants of Aaron who do not do the work of Aaron not go in peace" (*Yoma* 71b). Their comfort with their Gentile ancestry and their confidence in their current place in Jewish society must also have had its effect on Hillel.

No doubt Hillel was also welcoming to Gentiles interested in Judaism because he felt confident that the teachings of Judaism could bless the lives of non-Jews as well as of Jews, and that the Jewish community would be fortunate to augment its numbers with people attracted to its teachings. In short, he understood that it is possible to be a descendant of Aaron (who was one of Hillel's great heroes; see p. 70), and not be a good Jew, and equally possible to be of Gentile stock and be the worthy successor of Aaron.

I emphasize Hillel's unprecedented openness to converts because, in truth, all three of these men approached Hillel (and earlier Shammai) with such unreasonable demands that Hillel could easily have dismissed them. But it is clear that that is exactly what he did not want to do. When unreasonable conditions were thrown at him, he set out to see how he could still win the person over to Judaism.

What is also clear and even more striking is that the Talmud approves of Hillel's behavior and disapproves of Shammai's. Indeed, the Talmud gives the last words in the story not to Shammai or to Hillel, but to the three proselytes themselves: "Some time later, the three converts met in one place. They concluded: 'Shammai's great impatience sought to drive us from the world, but Hillel's gentleness brought us under the wings of the Divine Presence' " (*Shabbat* 31a).*

Yet a Fourth Talmudic Tale

In the stories told about the non-Jews who approach Hillel, none of the three is motivated to convert by the factor that motivates so many conversions today, the desire to marry a Jew. The rabbis were by no means unfamiliar with such a motivation, and it is the subject of one of the Talmud's most unusual, and certainly most romantic, stories. In this case, the rabbi involved was Rabbi Chiyya (late second century C.E.), who, like Hillel, was born in Babylonia and immigrated to Israel (see *Sanhedrin* 5a and *Ketubot* 5a), and who, again like Hillel, was referred to by the other rabbis as "the Babylonian" (*Genesis Rabbah* 26:4). Chiyya was the outstand-

---

* *The Fathers According to Rabbi Nathan* records that the convert who initially wanted to be High Priest subsequently had two sons, one of whom he named Hillel and the other Gamliel (the name of Hillel's grandson), and that these boys were known as the "proselytes of Hillel" (chap. 15).

ing student of Rabbi Judah the Prince, editor of the Mishnah and a direct descendant of Hillel. Chiyya's stature was such that the Talmud compares his achievements with those of Hillel: "At first, when Torah was forgotten from Israel, Ezra came up from Babylonia and reestablished it. Again, it was forgotten, and Hillel the Babylonian came and reestablished it. Again, it was forgotten and Rabbi Chiyya and his sons came up and reestablished it" (*Sukkah* 20a).

The Talmud relates that a student of Rabbi Chiyya's was particularly scrupulous in observing the law of tzitzit (ritual fringes). Nonetheless, when he heard of a beautiful prostitute in a far-off land who demanded four hundred gold coins as her price, he sent her the fee and set a date to meet her.

When the day arrived, he waited by the prostitute's door. Her maid came and told her, "The man who sent you four hundred gold coins is waiting at the door." The woman replied: "Let him come in."

When he entered . . . the prostitute went to her bed and lay down upon it naked. He too started toward her bed in his desire to sit naked with her when, all of a sudden, the four ritual fringes on his garment flew up and struck him across the face; at that point, he moved away from her and sat down on the ground.

The woman stepped down from her bed and sat down on the ground opposite him. "By the head of the Roman Empire," she swore, "I will not leave you alone until you tell me what blemish you saw in me [that caused you to leave my bed]."

He replied: "By the Temple, never have I seen a woman as beautiful as you are, but there is a commandment that the Lord our God has commanded us. It is called tzitzit." [He went on to explain that the fringes are intended to remind Jews to observe God's commandments; also, that God will reward those who keep His commandments and punish those who do not.] "Now the four fringes of the tzitzit appeared to me as four witnesses [testifying against me concerning the sin I was about to commit]."

The woman said: "I will not let you leave here until you tell me your name, the name of your town, the name of your teacher, and the name of the school in which you study Torah." He wrote all this down and put it in her hand. Thereupon [the man departed for home] and the woman divided her estate into three parts, one third to the Roman government, one third to be distributed among the poor, and the final third she [converted into jewelry and cash, which she] took with her. The linens on her bed, however, she kept. She then traveled to the yeshiva headed by Rabbi Chiyya, and said to him, "Master, instruct the rabbis to convert me to Judaism."

"My daughter," he replied, "perhaps you have set your eyes on one of my students?"

She took out the paper the young man had given her and handed it to Rabbi Chiyya. "Go," said he, "and enjoy your acquisition." [The woman was converted, and she married the young man. And so, the Talmud concludes]: "The very linens she had spread out for him for an illicit purpose, she now spread out for him lawfully." (*Menachot* 44a)

This story—which for obvious reasons is rarely taught in Jewish schools—suggests that romantic feelings leading to an interest in Judaism is not a uniquely modern phenomenon. Indeed, Rabbi Chiyya assumes that this is the woman's motive for wishing to convert. However, it quickly becomes clear that the man's Jewish values are crucial factors in the woman's being drawn to him, as indicated by her asking the man about his teacher and the school in which he studies. Although Rabbi Chiyya is correct in speculating that she has set her eyes on one of his students, he converts her because he believes that attraction to a Jew should not be a barrier to conversion, as long as the potential proselyte is also drawn to Judaism.

Rabbi Chiyya's precedent would seem to establish the principle that even if a non-Jew's initial interest in Judaism is stimulated by romance, that alone is not a reason to bar the person's conversion.*

---

* The nineteenth-century German rabbinic scholar David Tzvi Hoffman ruled that "if it is evident to the court that [the convert's] motivation is for the sake of heaven, even though he has set his eyes upon a Jewish woman, it is permissible to accept him" (*Melamed Le-Ho'il*, 2:83).

On Hillel, Chiyya, and the Jews of Today

Anxiety within Judaism about the place of converts has taken different forms at different moments in history. Questions of conversion cut to the heart of the "Who is a Jew?" question, one that, more than any other question in Jewish life, has the capability of turning intra-religious disagreements over conversion protocol into an outright separation that will divide Judaism not into movements like Reform, Conservative, Orthodox, and Reconstructionist but into truly schismatic denominations that will pull Jews apart from one another as much as Protestants and Catholics.

As a rabbi for almost forty years, I have seen the issue of conversion become an increasingly central concern in Jewish life. During my childhood in the 1950s, conversion was rarely discussed—certainly not in the traditional Jewish community in which I was raised—and rarely encouraged. Few Jews then were intermarrying. Until 1960, it is estimated that intermarriage rates were only about 6 percent. It is not that American Jews were necessarily so much more religious then than they are today, but even nonreligious Jews, many of them raised in Yiddish-speaking homes (as was very commonly the case in the 1920s and 1930s), were unlikely to be so socially at ease with non-Jews that they would marry them (non-Jews apparently felt the same).

Those days are long past. Jews today live among non-Jews

in a way they didn't previously. Two generations ago, for example, Jews who attended college generally studied at public universities and lived at home (in the 1930s, CCNY, the City College of New York, was estimated to have a student body that was more than 80 percent Jewish). In contrast, many young Jews today attend residential colleges and graduate schools (and, later, accept jobs) far from their homes and, not surprisingly, often fall in love with non-Jewish peers whom they meet there.

Since the 1970s, intermarriage rates in the Diaspora have grown to more than 40 percent, and it is now clear that unless Jews find ways to bring the non-Jewish spouses of Jews, and the children of intermarried couples, into the Jewish community, the Jewish population will decline precipitously. In 1938, just before World War II, the worldwide Jewish population was estimated at 17 million, or more than three-quarters of 1 percent of a world population of some 2.2 billion. As of 2009, the world's population had more than tripled, to about 6.8 billion, while Jewry's numbers had fallen to about 14 milion, or less than one-quarter of 1 percent of the world's population. The decline both in absolute numbers and in Jews as a percentage of the population over the past seventy years is due in large measure, of course, to the Holocaust. But not only to the Holocaust. In the United States, a country in which (aside from American Jews serving in the military) no Jews died because of Nazi persecution, Jews have gone from 4 percent of the population to under 2 percent today. And all this despite large post–World War II migrations of Holocaust survivors, Israelis, and Jews from Russia, Iran, and South Africa (in contrast, an average of 2,000 to 3,000 Jews leave the United States annually to live in Israel).

Two thousand years ago, Judaism—from which Christianity sprang and from which Muhammad acknowledged that he first learned about God—was the world's only monotheist faith. Christianity was just beginning, and Islam would not come into existence for another six hundred years. Today, not only is Judaism the smallest of the three monotheist faiths, but there are more than a hundred Christians (including Catholics, Protestants, and adherents of the Orthodox churches) and almost a hundred Muslims for every Jew.

There is little risk of the Jewish people in the Dispora disappearing altogether; there are strong centers of committed Jews who seem to be in no risk from either physical destruction or assimilation. But in many societies, Jews run the risk of becoming so small in numbers that they will become numerically insignificant and eventually inconsequential.* In the United States, where Jews have long numbered between 5 million and 6 million, they have exerted a great impact and are recognized as an important religious and ethnic group. But if the Jewish decline as a percentage of the population continues (along with a decline in numbers), and Jews eventually become 1 percent, or even a half percent, of the American people, their impact on society will obviously decline as well.

---

* In India and China, for example, the world's two most populous countries, Jews have long numbered in the low thousands and are barely noticed at all.

There are, I am aware, many Jews (overwhelmingly concentrated in the observant community) who strongly oppose a policy of encouraging conversion to Judaism, believing that it is forbidden to admit anyone who is romantically involved with a Jew and anyone who does not undertake a long course of study and a commitment to observe Jewish law "in toto." Rabbi Marc Angel, a prominent Orthodox rabbi in New York (and a man who himself favors a somewhat more open approach to would-be converts), writes of a lecture on "practical rabbinics" given by a leading Talmud scholar at RIETS, the Orthodox seminary at Yeshiva University, in which the scholar instructed the soon-to-be-ordained rabbis not to perform a conversion unless they were willing to bet $100,000 of their own money that the convert would observe all Jewish laws. One student asked, "Since no one can guarantee absolutely the future of any convert, doesn't this mean that Orthodox rabbis should avoid performing conversions?"* After hemming and hawing, the rabbi suggested that Orthodox rabbis should never, or only rarely, perform conversions.

It is in the context of such responses that it is so refreshing—and surprising—to turn to Hillel, the most traditional of Jews with the most untraditional of views, whose ideas on conversion resonate with twenty-first-century Jewish life more than with any century since he lived. When

---

* A friend of mine, a physician and himself an Orthodox Jew, notes that, by this logic, no surgeon would ever operate, since if an operation doesn't succeed to the extent the patient hoped and the doctor expected, the physician might well be sued for malpractice. The only way to avoid this is to never operate. Clearly, that would not be good.

someone approached Hillel with an interest in becoming Jewish, his inclination was to bring the person in. Obviously, the goal of conversion is to generate a substantial commitment to Jewish values, traditions, and laws, as well as to the meaningfulness of the study of Jewish texts. Without that, Rabbi Saul Berman notes, "we run the risk of producing a people without the vision necessary to impact on the world, and it is hard to believe that this is what Hillel was promoting." For long centuries, the inclination of rabbis has been to emphasize the difficulties of being Jewish, to teach that Judaism is not interested in non-Jews assuming a Jewish identity, and to discourage converts (some rabbis even insist that a person be strongly turned away three times).[7] All that this strategy will guarantee today is that Jews will become a smaller and smaller people, much less capable of using Jewish tradition to make an impact on the world. Hillel did not want that, and neither should we.

5

Repairing the World

We can only speculate as to why Hillel was remarkably open to converts. We can guess about his upbringing, the example of his teachers—descended from converts—or the shaping influence of his own experience as an outsider, a Babylonian among Jerusalemites, a poor man among the wealthy. But we can only guess.

We do know that his view of converts was of a piece with his larger understanding of the primacy of the ethical treatment of one's fellow human beings. There is a concept first identified with Hillel that offers a tantalizing glimpse of what might almost be called his theological philosophy. That concept is *tikkun olam*, a phrase that literally means "repairing the world," although it is sometimes translated as "perfecting the world" or "bettering the world."

Tikkun olam is one of relatively few Hebrew phrases that is widely known even among Jews whose knowledge of Hebrew is limited. But long before its absorption by contemporary Jews who have made it a kind of Hebrew analogue for what is sometimes called "social justice," it was employed two thousand years ago by Hillel to justify one of the most radical moves ever made by a Talmudic sage. Hillel invoked it to argue successfully for an all but heretical act—the effective overturning of a Torah law in the name of compassion.

What makes this story so astonishing and even today vaguely controversial is that, then as now, the first place religious Jews looked for guidelines on how to bring about the world's improvement was the Torah's laws. What happens, though, when the Torah enacts a law to help people, but the law's strict fulfillment ends up hurting them instead? This was precisely the dilemma that Hillel confronted on two occasions, and it is he—and this is not widely remembered today—who first utilized the principle of *tikkun olam* as a rationale for modifying a Torah law.

The words of Paul in 2 Corinthians (3:6), "The letter killeth but the spirit giveth life," has long echoed harshly in Jewish ears, and for good reason. What it came to mean in the Western mind is that law-bound Jews are soulless literalists, and Christians are animated by the spirit of God. Paul's words were, in fact, a great outreach tool to pagans, who were invited to participate in the promise of the Torah unencumbered by Jewish law.

But the argument of letter and spirit fits firmly inside Jewish thinking—not as an either/or proposition but as a question of integration. Hillel, who took Jewish law with the utmost seriousness, was arguing for spirit over letter in a famous instance involving the sensitive issue of canceling debts, but never—as Paul did—for the abrogation of Torah law in general.

According to biblical law, every seven years debts due on personal loans are canceled: "Every seventh year you shall practice remission [i.e., forgiving] of debts. This shall be the nature of the remission: every creditor shall remit the amount that he claims from his fellow; he shall not exact it of his neighbor or kinsman, for the remission proclaimed is of the Lord" (Deut. 15:1–2). The economy of Israel in its earliest days was overwhelmingly agricultural (as was true of most of the world) and dependent on barter. In such societies, money was generally needed only for dire emergencies, and the people reduced to borrowing money were most often the poor. If the debts incurred could not be repaid, the results would be catastrophic, involving, for example, confiscation of the borrower's land. The Torah's concern was to prevent such occurrences and the creation thereby of a permanent poor class. Every seventh year, therefore, a person was given an opportunity to start over.

From a lender's perspective, the cancellation of the debt was, to say the least, annoying. But in truth, at a time when there were no conventional charitable institutions such as soup kitchens, loaning money to the poor (and such loans were interest-free; see Exod. 22:24) was also one of the major forms of charity. Well aware that the cancellation of debts would alienate many potential lenders, the Torah warned people: "Do not harden your heart and shut your hand against your needy kinsman. Rather you must open your hand and lend him sufficient for whatever he needs. Beware lest you harbor the base thought, 'The seventh year, the year of remission [of debts] is approaching,' so that you are mean to your needy kinsman and give him nothing. He will cry out to the Lord against you, and you will incur guilt" (Deut. 15:7–10).

We have no way of knowing how well the Torah's legislation and warnings worked in Israel's earliest years in securing loans for the poor. Did people really refrain from allowing "base thoughts" to discourage them from making loans? Probably some tenderhearted people, realizing that those in need of cash were truly in desperate straits, went ahead and made such loans, but many others likely didn't.[1]

By the time of Hillel, the economy of ancient Israel was becoming an urban as well as an agricultural one. In an urban, money-oriented economy, more people require loans. Unfortunately, not enough people were willing to lend money interest-free and, in addition, run the risk of having their loans canceled. Particularly as the seventh year of the cycle drew near, fewer and fewer loans were extended. This was the dilemma confronting Hillel. Now, because of this law, *intended to help the poor*, fewer people were willing to make loans, and the application of Torah law under these new circumstances was undermining the ethical purpose of the very law itself. In short, the Torah law in this instance was undermining the Torah ethic.

Hillel, the Mishnah writes, "saw that people refrained from giving loans one to another." But what was he, as the leading rabbinic figure of his age, to do? To simply declare that the Torah law, though noble in intent, was now void was not an option; Torah law is understood in Jewish tradition as being eternally binding and not subject to abrogation. What Hillel did take advantage of—and in this regard his solution was both innovative and courageous—is that the Torah law canceling debts was never understood in Jewish law as applying to *all* debts. For example, if you owed money to a laborer, you were not freed from the debt simply because the seven-year cycle arrived. Similarly, debts incurred to a shopkeeper were still binding. And, most important from Hillel's perspective, "payments fixed by court action [in other words, money due to a court] are not canceled" (see Mishnah *Shvi'it* 10:1–2).

Hillel therefore instituted the procedure known as *prozbol*, a document by which a lender transferred a debt due him into one owed to the court. The man would bring evidence of the loan before judges who would affirm the lender's right, as agent of the court, to collect the debt, even during and after the seventh year.

In theory, the Torah law canceling personal debts in the seventh year was still applicable; in practice, though, it was no longer observed. Hillel's rationale for doing so was *tikkun olam:* "Hillel the Elder enacted the *prozbol* to make the world better *(mipnei tikkun olam)* because he saw that people refrained from lending money to one another and violated what was written in the Torah, 'lest you harbor the base thought' " (*Sifri*, *Re'eh* 113).

Hundreds of years later, sages continued to debate the audacity of Hillel's enactment: "Is it possible that where the Torah requires a cancellation of debts Hillel ordains that there not be a cancellation?" (*Gittin* 36b; the commentator Rashi adds, "and thus uproots an injunction of the Torah").

One sage, Shmuel, feeling that this is exactly what Hillel did, went so far as to say, "If I am ever in a position to do so, I will abolish [the *prozbol*]." But Rabbi Nachman responded that the *prozbol* was a permanent feature of Jewish life, and that it now applied even in instances where no document was written. All debts, whether brought before judges or not, were automatically transferred in the seventh year to the courts, and remained collectible (*Gittin* 36b). But, according to Jewish law, the *prozbol* document still needs to be written, and observant Jews do so.

It may be possible to glimpse in the later controversy around Hillel's invocation of *tikkun olam*—a controversy taking place long after the destruction of the Temple and the rise of Christianity—an aspect of what has made Hillel's openness so uncomfortable for contemporary, post-Holocaust, traditional Jews. What ultimately separates Judaism from Christianity—aside from the glaring difference of opinion about the Messiah and about the divine status certain passages in the New Testament assign to Jesus—is the difference of opinion about the binding nature of Torah law. As more Jews drift away from observance of the law, anxiety about what keeps the two groups separate has only grown in some quarters. Hillel's openness to converts may now be viewed as one more step toward eroding the distinctions, when of course it was born out of strength and confidence in Judaism's ultimate power to transform those who join its ranks.

A second enactment of Hillel was likewise intended to protect the needy, this time from the hands of unscrupulous purchasers who used the letter of Torah law to thwart its intentions. A biblical law, widely unknown today, stated, "If a man sells a dwelling place in a walled city, it may be redeemed [that is, bought back] until a year has elapsed since its sale. . . . If it is not redeemed before a full year has elapsed, the house in the walled city shall pass to the purchaser beyond reclaim throughout the ages" (Lev. 25:29–30). In other words, the seller of the house has exactly a year to buy it back; otherwise, he loses ownership of it forever.

What was the reason for this strange-sounding law, allowing a seller to buy back his house within a specified time period? Nachmanides, the thirteenth-century Bible commentator, explains: "Inasmuch as the sale of a person's house is an act of extreme gravity, and he is humiliated when he sells it, the Torah sought to have him redeem it during his first year."

The Torah law is clear. As long as the seller can come up with the money to redeem his house within a year, he can take the sum to the purchaser and not lose what is, in all likelihood, a long-standing family dwelling. But, the Mishnah explains, some purchasers would seek to evade this law by hiding themselves on the last day or days of the twelfth month, so that the seller could not find them to give them the money. Then, as soon as the day ended and the year elapsed, they would emerge from hiding and take permanent possession of the home. Thus, the house would have been acquired in a technically legal way, but in clear contravention of the Torah's intention.

How to deal with this? Again, Hillel did not feel that he,

or any one, had the right to simply declare that the Torah law restricting the seller's right to buy back the house to twelve months no longer applied, and that the seller now had unlimited time in which to redeem his house. Such an enactment would not only have voided a Torah law, it also would have been unfair to purchasers, including those who were not tricksters, for it would mean that no matter how long they occupied the house, the seller would always have the option of coming with the money and taking back possession.

How, therefore, to be fair to sellers and purchasers alike?

In an innovative act, Hillel turned the treasury at the Temple into a part-time business office, ruling that the former owner could, within the year, take the money to redeem his house to the Temple. The Temple in turn would hold the money for the buyer. Meanwhile, the former owner, instead of having to go on an ultimately hopeless chase after the hiding purchaser, could now, in the words of the Mishnah, "break down the door" and reenter the house he had been forced to sell, but which was now his once more (Mishnah *Arakhin* 9:4).

There are unscrupulous people who use the full range of their intellect to figure out how to remain within the technical boundaries of the law while still being able to cheat people. Then there are those who throw up their hands at such behavior and say, "Of course what they are doing is disgusting. But it's in the nature of law that there will always be some people who exploit it to their advantage, and there isn't anything that we can do about it." In Hillel, these sorts of unscrupulous people met their match—a man who could be sly as they, only in this case out of a desire to protect the innocent from oppression while abiding by the letter of the law. We see in this type of behavior a fulfillment of Hillel's own dictum, "In a place where there are no men [willing to take action], try to be a man" (*Ethics of the Fathers* 2:6): Do the right thing, for if you don't, people's lives will be diminished rather than elevated by the Torah.

I understand Hillel's usage of the concept of *tikkun olam* as intended to create a safeguard against the dangers of legalism. Ironically, religions are endangered not only by external threats, but sometimes by their endemic strengths as well. One of Judaism's great strengths is its halakhic (legal) system, its concretization of Judaism's ideals into law. It isn't enough to tell people to not go about as gossips (Lev. 19:16); Jewish law offers very specific regulations on what constitutes speaking unfairly about others and what things are permitted and what things are not permitted to be said. This is the strength of a legal tradition; it insists that people turn noble but potentially abstract ideals (like "love your neighbor as yourself") into righteous deeds, and offers them a standard for doing so.

But the problem confronting a legal tradition is that the law can become an end unto itself. Consider, for example, a discussion in the Talmud (*Kiddushin* 31a) of the fifth commandment, "Honor your father and your mother." On the one hand, it is striking that in the first legal document legislated for the entire Israelite people, such emphasis is placed on honoring one's parents, and there is no question that this early emphasis on familial obligations has characterized Jewish life ever since.

On the other hand, when you examine some Talmudic texts defining what it means to honor your parents, the demands become quite extreme. When Rabbi Tarfon noted with pride that he would bend over so his mother could step on his back to comfortably ascend to or descend from her bed, his rabbinic colleagues said to him, "You haven't yet reached half the honor due to a mother. Have you let your mother throw your money into the sea without doing anything to [restrain her or] embarrass her?" (*Kiddushin* 31b). The third-century sage, Rabbi Yonatan, despairing of the possibility of ever obeying the law to honor one's parents properly, finally declares, "Happy is the person who has never seen his parents."* This statement epitomizes the dangers confronting a legalistic religion: a rabbi ends up declaring that it is better to be an orphan, because that way one will not be punished for violating a series of laws that can never be fulfilled properly.[2]

Hillel understood that if Judaism defined itself exclusively by literal observance of Torah law, it would end up, for example, with poor people unable to secure loans, even though securing loans is exactly what the Torah wanted to see happen. The law itself, he understood, requires a principle of *tikkun olam*, a standard that can be used to moderate

---

* Rashi explains Rabbi Yonatan's comment: since it is impossible to fulfill the commandment to honor one's parents in all its details, a child will inevitably be punished on account of them.

and modify the law when it is not achieving the goal it was intended to achieve. It is obvious that something has gone wrong if the very law mandating the honoring of one's parents turns this filial obligation into so onerous a task that a great rabbi can end up declaring that it is preferable to be an orphan.* Preferable for whom? The child? The parents? This is what can happen if the law comes to be seen as an end in itself, divorced from intention and common sense.

Once introduced, the concept of *tikkun olam* continued to be utilized when there was danger that following the strict letter of the law would end up damaging people in ways that the law never intended. For example, the biblical and rabbinic belief in the great value of human life prompted the rabbis to declare that all Jewish laws (with three exceptions)[3] should be suspended to save a life. This is the basis for the ruling that violating Judaism's most sacred holidays, such as the Shabbat and Yom Kippur, is permissible in such an instance (see pp. 5–6).

Similarly, because of the value of life, the rabbis rule that when a Jew is kidnapped and held for ransom—and whose life is more at risk than a captive in such a situation?—the Jewish community is obligated to raise the money to free him. But just how much should be paid? Any sum necessary, one might argue, because human life is of infinite value. In actuality, because of the principle of *tikkun olam*, limits are

* My daughter Shira Telushkin has noted that coming to regard the commandment of honor for parents as a burden and an obstacle ironically leads to disrespect for parents, for what could be more disrespectful than wishing one was freed from this obligation?

placed on how much should be spent. The Mishnah rules: "One does not ransom captives for more than their value because of *tikkun olam*" (Mishnah *Gittin* 4:6). The Talmud offers two reasons for this restriction: First, so that kidnappers do not seize more captives. If it is known that Jews pay more than other groups to save their members, brigands will target Jews and all Jews will be at risk. As Maimonides writes: "We do not redeem captives for more than their worth . . . so that enemies will not pursue people to hold them captive" ("Laws of Gifts to the Poor" 8:12). Alternatively, or in addition, it is forbidden to pay excessive amounts to redeem captives because doing so may end up impoverishing the community.

To this day, the concept of *tikkun olam*, first associated with Hillel, continues to have enduring relevance. Whether it is in a discussion of what price Israel should pay to redeem kidnapped soldiers (including releasing convicted terrorists who might then harm and murder others) or of whether governments and insurance companies should expend enormous sums caring for ill people with limited possibilities of recovery (and thereby run the risk of impoverishing the community), this principle ensures that the Torah ethic can be applied even in new, unanticipated circumstances. Hillel's delicate balancing act—sustaining the Torah ethic without formally voiding a Torah law—helped the needy Jews of Hillel's time, and has helped the Jewish people ever since.[4]

6

Five Traits

ikkun olam is a lofty concept, but Hillel, like rabbinic Judaism itself, was deeply concerned with the daily behavior of human beings. The modern notion of scholarship is alien to the world of traditional Torah study, where practice and learning are braided together, and nobody exemplifies this more than Hillel. Writing about Hillel, reading about him, is not a passive activity. There is a way in which he is constantly reaching out of the stories in which he has come down to us, opening his door and welcoming us in as if we ourselves were the potential converts, or strangers, or poor men at the door. He teaches through precepts but also understood that behavior is in itself a lesson—a lesson that says, as it did to the converts whose lives he altered: "You must change your life." He not only tells us, "The rest is commentary, now go and study," but, through his actions, he shows us that "the rest is behavior, now go and do."

For this reason, we might well ask what Hillel's daily life was like. We can, alas, only guess. The Talmud gives us glimpses, but biography has never been a Jewish form. The

Chafetz Chayyim, the subject of the beautiful story of righteousness with which this book began, lived into the twentieth century, but his very name—Israel Meir Kagan—has been eclipsed by the name of one of his books. Hillel has retained his own name, but his actions, and the lessons implicit in them, seem missing at times from our understanding of his greatness and his contemporary relevance. And just as his openness to non-Jews wishing to convert is honored but ignored, so his individual qualities, as they are represented in the stories that have come down to us, seem in need of rescue.

To that end, I have distilled five aspects of Hillel's personality: his patience, his moral imagination, his optimism, his nonjudgmental nature, and his intense curiosity. These are, in fact, the very traits that enabled his openness to all whom he met.

Extreme Patience

> It is worth it that you should lose 400 *zuzim* and yet
> another 400 *zuzim*, but Hillel shall not become angry.
> —*Shabbat* 31a

In the Talmud, Hillel's patience is, quite literally, legendary. To illustrate it, the Talmud tells a story about gambling, which is in itself unusual because there is only one bet that I can think of that is mentioned in the entire Talmud.

While the prevailing view in Jewish sources is that gambling is permitted, earning one's living as a full-time gambler is regarded as disreputable. Such a person is seen by some rabbis as untrustworthy, and by others as one who does nothing productive for the world. The Talmud therefore rules that a full-time gambler (though not an occasional one) is disqualified from serving as a witness before a Jewish court (see Mishnah *Sanhedrin* 3:3).

This brings us to the lone bet I recall from the Talmud.[1] Strangely enough, it involves—if only indirectly—Hillel. Apparently, his patience was a source of fame even during his lifetime, and two men bet each other 400 *zuzim* (an enormous sum of money at the time, given that the amount of money a man had to compensate his wife if he divorced her was only 200 *zuzim*) that one of them could provoke Hillel's anger.

It was Friday, just before the Sabbath, when people are very rushed. Hillel was washing his head. One of the men passed by the door of Hillel's house and called out, "Is Hillel here? Is Hillel here?"

Hillel put on a robe and went out to him, saying, "My son, what do you want?"

"I have a question to ask," said the man.

"Ask, my son," Hillel prompted.

The man said, "Why are the heads of the Babylonians round?"[2]

Hillel replied, "My son, you have asked a great question. It is because they have no skilled midwives."

The man departed, waited awhile, returned, and called out, "Is Hillel here? Is Hillel here?"

Hillel again put on a robe and went out to him, saying, "My son, what do you want?"

"I have a question to ask," the man said.

"Ask, my son," Hillel said.

The man asked, "Why are the eyes of the Palmyreans bleary?"

Hillel answered. "My son, you have asked a great question. It is because they live in sandy places."

The man departed, waited awhile, returned, and called out, "Is Hillel here? Is Hillel here?"

Hillel again put on his robe, went out to him, and said, "My son, what do you want?"

"I have a question to ask," said the man.

Hillel told him, "Ask, my son."

The man asked, "Why are the feet of Africans wide?"

Said Hillel, "My son, you have asked a great question. It is because they live in watery marshes."

The man said, "I have many question to ask, but fear that you may become angry." Thereupon, Hillel sat down before him and said, "Ask all the questions you have to ask."

The man said, "Are you the Hillel who is called the *nasi* [president or leader] of Israel?"

"Yes," Hillel replied.

"If that is so," the man said, "may there not be many like you in Israel."

"Why, my son?" Hillel asked.

The man answered, "Because on account of you I have lost four hundred *zuzim*" [and he proceeded to explain to Hillel about the bet he had made].

Hillel answered him. "Be careful of your moods. It is worth it that you should lose four hundred *zuzim* and yet another four hundred *zuzim*, but Hillel shall not become angry" [literally, "not take offense"] (*Shabbat* 31a).

While Hillel's explanation of the Babylonians' round heads and the Africans' wide feet might not pass muster with anthropologists or biologists, Rabbi Adin Steinsaltz notes that these responses are consistent with Hillel's generally humanistic teachings and his focus on the commonality of people: "[Hillel believed that] racial diversity is the result not of essential differences but, by and large, of circumstances and conditions."[3]

Although the impression we have from Hillel's many aphorisms is generally one of passionate moderation (see, for example, pp. 164–167), in two areas he is depicted as extreme: in the previously cited instance of his devotion to Torah learning (how many people would run the risk of freezing to death to hear a Torah lecture) and in his refusal to allow himself to lose his temper. Perhaps great equanimity came naturally to him, or perhaps Hillel, aware that his rival Shammai was known for unrestrained bursts of anger—he chased away two would-be converts with a stick—felt the need to model a never-ending patience.

Nonetheless, and whatever might be the explanation, this incident does seem a bit extreme. Elie Wiesel has commented that "the anecdotes about Hillel's patience finally put a strain on mine."[4] But perhaps the Talmud records this story to teach us that there is little that human beings cannot control if they are sufficiently determined. True, it is not always wrong to lose one's temper, and we can find many examples in the Bible where a loss of temper is seen as justified. For example, God is outraged at Balaam for misusing his prophetic talents by taking money from the king of Moab to curse the Israelites (Num. 22:22); Jacob is viewed as justified in expressing great anger to his father-in-law Laban for his lack of gratitude (Gen. 31:36–42); and Moses is outraged by the rebels Korach, Datan, and Abiram for slandering him with the claim that he used his position of leadership to enrich himself (Num. 16:15). That God and figures such as Jacob and Moses all express anger indicates that, when directed fairly and at justified targets, feeling and verbalizing anger can be the moral thing to do.

Similarly, a Mishnaic passage justifies occasional expressions of anger by speaking of a *saintly* person as one who is "difficult to anger and easy to appease" (*Ethics of the Fathers* 5:11). The Talmud does not say, "impossible to anger," just "difficult." Hillel, however, chooses to model a standard bordering on the impossible, and while this is not a standard that can be demanded from everyone, he was willing to demand it of himself.

Perhaps those of us prone to explosions of anger and cutting retorts can look to Hillel for guidance. We may not achieve the almost complete cessation of anger he did,[5] but a 50 percent improvement might well bless the lives of those who deal with us. If you are a *kapdan*, of hotheaded disposition, ask your family members, your students, or your employees if they would be unhappy if you reduced your expressions of anger or your cutting comments by 50 percent.

Such a statement might provoke a variety of responses. What it will not provoke, however, is an argument.

Moral Imagination

Hillel provided a horse for the [formerly rich] man to ride upon.

—*Ketubot* 67b

That Hillel allowed himself to freeze under more than four feet of snow while lying on the roof of Shmaya and Avtalion's yeshiva might suggest to some that he was of an ascetic temperament. Such a view would be further reinforced by Hillel's refusal to accept financial support—at a time when he was poor—from his brother, Shebna, who seems to have been a successful businessman (*Sotah* 21a).

On the other hand, at a time when standards of personal hygiene were low, Hillel made great efforts to remain clean. Indeed, he seemed to take genuine enjoyment from some basic bodily pleasures. The Midrash records that on one occasion, Hillel concluded a class with his disciples and left the House of Study together with them.

The disciples asked him where he was going, and Hillel answered, "To fulfill a religious obligation."

"Which religious obligation?" they asked.

"I am going to the bathhouse to take a bath."

The astonished disciples asked, "Is that really a religious obligation?"

Hillel answered: "Yes! If somebody who is appointed to scrape and clean the statues of the king that stand in the theaters and circuses is paid for the work and even associates with the nobility, how much more should I, who am created in the image and likeness of God . . . take care of my body?" (*Leviticus Rabbah* 34:3).

Hillel is teaching his disciples that, while the study they have been engaged in is of great importance, the body and its care matter, too. Leviticus 19:18 may instruct us to love our neighbors as ourselves, but if we do not love ourselves, how good are we going to be at loving our neighbors? His justification—that we are made in the image of God— is also of course a key to understanding the basis of his treatment of outsiders. He reasoned from his own body outward—the opposite of a narcissist—and recognized that caring for others is also caring for God.

But it is the very embodied nature of his thinking that allowed him to make room for the individual. Just as all bodies are different—some have round heads, some have flat feet—they are all made equally in God's image.

Although Hillel chose a life of simplicity for himself (in one of his aphorisms, he taught, "One who increases his possessions, increases his worries" [*Ethics of the Fathers* 2:7]), he was nonjudgmental and understanding of the wants of others. A biblical verse commands Jews to give a poor person "sufficient for his needs" (Deut. 15:8). The standard understanding of this phrase is offered in the *Shulchan Arukh:* "If he is hungry, he should be fed. If he needs clothes, he should be provided with clothes. If he has no household furniture or utensils, furniture and utensils should be provided" (*Yoreh De'ah* 250:1).

But the Talmud offers another interpretation of "sufficient for his needs": that when dispensing charity, you take into account the recipient's emotional as well as physical needs and desires. For example, a rich person who becomes impoverished should be maintained at a higher level than one who has always been poor, because for such a person the descent into poverty likely causes greater suffering than for one who has never known anything better. In the context of commenting on the verse in Deuteronomy, the Talmud relates an anecdote about Hillel, who might well have been the first person to express concern about the treatment of the formerly rich. "They said about Hillel the Elder that he undertook the care of a poor man from an aristocratic family. Hillel provided a horse for the man to ride upon, and a servant to accompany him [literally, 'to run before him']. On one occasion, Hillel could not find a servant to accompany the man, so he ran before him for three *millin* [about two miles]" (*Ketubot* 67b).

There is no evidence that Hillel, even after he became the religious leader of his age, owned a horse or that he had servants working in his household. The one story we know about Hillel's wife suggests that she had no help in the kitchen (see p. 101). Yet Hillel had the moral imagination to understand that while *he* might not need a horse, this man from so different a background might, and might even require the luxury of a servant.[6] Would Hillel expect the community to provide the poor man with this expensive lifestyle forever? Perhaps not. Perhaps he understood that the man just needed time to gradually adjust to his new economic status. And Hillel wanted to give him that time.[7]

Hillel understood that "love your neighbor as yourself" does not always mean that we should want precisely the same thing for our neighbor as we want for ourselves. Sometimes it means that for our neighbor we should want, and provide, more.

Optimism

Leave it to the people. If they are not themselves prophets, they are the children of prophets.

—*Pesachim* 66a

There was a lightness of spirit in Hillel's approach to people, and a calmness in his responses to situations that might, in others, prompt anxiety. This may of course have been merely a matter of the mystery of temperament, but it seems symbolic of an idea about Judaism itself, an idea that would grow more difficult to sustain in the centuries following the destruction of the Temple, when the Jews were scattered throughout the world and other monotheistic religions born of Judaism gained global dominance.

Earlier, I cited the case in which a question was raised regarding a person who forgot to bring a knife with him to the Temple before the Sabbath, which that year corresponded with the beginning of Passover. Carrying a knife on

the Sabbath is forbidden, but it would be a great hardship to
be without the knife because it would then be impossible to
perform the Passover sacrifice. Hillel responded with equanimity: "I have heard what this law is, but I have forgotten
it. However, leave it to the people. If they are not themselves prophets, they are the children of prophets" (*Pesachim*
66a). I don't know if there are many other rabbis who would
have calmly entrusted such a major decision to the masses.
The following day, the people justified Hillel's confidence in
them and provided a solution that enabled them to bring the
needed knives to the Temple without violating Jewish law
(see p. 16).

As an optimist, Hillel, it seems, had a greater capacity
than Shammai to take pleasure in the moment. Thus, the
Talmud describes Shammai's devotion to properly honoring
the Sabbath: "They said about Shammai the Elder that
every day he would eat in honor of the Sabbath. How so? If
he came across a superior animal that could be eaten, he
would say, 'This should be set aside for the Sabbath meal.'
Then, if he later came across an ever better animal, he would
set aside that one for the Sabbath, and eat the first during
the week." Thus, the Talmud credits Shammai with honoring the Sabbath even during the week, since he would eat
inferior meals on weekdays so that he could save superior
food for the Sabbath. But Hillel the Elder, the Talmud continues, had an altogether different mind-set: on any given
day, he would simply eat whatever food was available. Unlike
Shammai, Hillel appeared confident that he would find
appropriate food for Shabbat when the time came. The rab-

bis applied to him the verse, "Blessed be God day by day" (Pss. 68:20), which Hillel understood to mean that he not be unduly concerned with what might or might not be available in a few days' time (see *Beitzah* 16a).

One particular difference of opinion between the schools of Hillel and Shammai reveals their differing perspectives on human nature, and also reflects an optimistic versus a more pessimistic mind-set. The School of Shammai restricted attendance at its academy to people who were already wise and humble (one wonders if people asked themselves before applying to Shammai's school, "Am I sufficiently humble to be worthy of admission?") and who came from a distinguished background. In contrast, the School of Hillel was willing to admit all applicants into the *Beit Midrash* (House of Study)—just as Hillel was more willing than Shammai to admit people into the Jewish community (for more on this dispute and its implications for contemporary Jewish behavior, see chapter 13).

Optimism concerning others' potential generally coincides with a loving attitude toward them. And so it is not a surprise that Hillel's biblical hero is Aaron, Moses's brother and Israel's first High Priest. In Jewish tradition, Aaron is enshrined as someone permeated with love for his fellow man. The rabbis tell the following story concerning him:

> When two men had quarreled, Aaron would go and sit with one of them and say, "My son, see what your friend is doing! He beats his breast and tears his clothes and moans, 'Woe is me! How can I lift my eyes and look

my companion in the face? I am ashamed before him, since it is I who treated him foully.' "

Aaron would sit with him until he had removed all anger [literally, jealousy] from his heart.

Then Aaron would go and sit with the other man and say likewise, "My son, see what your friend is doing! He beats his breast and tears his clothes and moans, 'Woe is me! How can I lift my eyes and look my companion in the face? I am ashamed before him since it was I who offended him.' "

Aaron would sit with him also until he had removed all anger from his heart.

Later, when the two met, they would embrace and kiss each other. (*The Fathers According to Rabbi Nathan* 12:3)

Aaron is the sole biblical character to whom Hillel refers in the many aphorisms attributed to him in *Ethics of the Fathers:* "Be of the disciples of Aaron, loving peace and pursuing peace, loving people and drawing them near to the Torah" (*Ethics of the Fathers* 1:12).

In contrast to Hillel, Shammai and his followers do not appear to have been interested in winning over to Jewish commitment people who were not already committed. But if they were already wise, humble, and from distinguished families, Shammai stood ready to teach them. Not so with Hillel; to him, Jews, non-Jews, righteous people, sinners— all could be won over to a life of Jewish learning, commitment, and goodness.

Nonjudgmental Nature

Do not judge your fellow until you are in his place.
—HILLEL, *Ethics of the Fathers* 2:4

Perhaps the most ignored of the Torah's 613 command-ments is "In justice you shall judge your fellow man" (Lev. 19:15). In addition to instructing judges to be scrupulously fair—for example, not to favor the rich over the poor or the poor over the rich (Lev. 19:15)—this verse is understood in Jewish law as applying to every person and to nonjudicial settings as well. We are all called upon to judge one another fairly.

Almost all of us make judgments about people every day, and often our judgments are critical and harsh. Our children do not immediately do something we request of them, and we condemn them, verbally, or in our minds, as selfish or never listening to us, even though many times in a day they do obey us, even when we ask them to do something they might not want to.[8] A waiter at a restaurant serves us more slowly than we would like or makes an error in bringing our order, and we find ourselves reaching all sorts of unwarranted and condemnatory conclusions about the person.

If we tend to be unduly judgmental even in instances where someone has simply done something annoying, rather than truly wrong, we are even more apt to be judgmental when there is actual evidence of wrongdoing. It is concerning *such* cases that Hillel issues his somewhat surprising appeal: "Do not judge your fellow until you are in his place." According to the Talmud, idolatry is regarded as one of the three worst sins (up there with murder and the most serious sexual offenses). But even in such a case, the rabbis were not entirely without understanding for those who engaged in such behavior. The Talmud relates that during a public lecture, Rabbi Ashi made a sarcastic reference to the idolatrous king Menashe, a long-dead monarch. That night, Menashe appeared to Ashi in a dream. The king posed a difficult question in Jewish law to the rabbi, and when Ashi couldn't answer it, Menashe did. The startled rabbi not only assured the king that he would repeat the question and answer to his class the following day, but then asked him, "Since you are so learned, why did you worship idols?" Menashe answered, "Had you been there, you would have lifted up the bottom of your garment and run after me" (*Sanhedrin* 102b). Idolatry might be a horrid offense, and we are right to condemn it; nonetheless, we should still seek to understand why another—and perhaps we ourselves—might be seduced into engaging in it.*

* In yet another Talmudic passage, this is precisely what rabbis do. Commenting on the biblical characters Chananiah, Mishael, and Azariah (commonly known by the names assigned them by the Babylonians, Shadrach, Meshach, and Abednego), who were willing to suffer martyrdom rather than engage in idolatry, the Talmudic rabbi Rav says, "Had they lashed Chananiah, Mishael, and Azariah, they would have worshipped the statue" (*Ketubot* 33b). In other words, even those who might be willing to be martyrs might not be able to stand up to torture.

The sort of wisdom articulated in the Talmud's approach carries over into daily life and into unexpected professions. My friend Howard Fine, one

One might say that Hillel's great insight was that if any Jew might, under different circumstances, be an idol worshipper, perhaps any idol worshipper could eventually become a Jew. In order to reach this conclusion, imagination is certainly necessary. But so is a suspension of judgment, the easy condemnation of people based on appearances.

M y friend Dr. Isaac Herschkopf shared with me a recollection about a time when he was too quick to judge another harshly:

> I remember sitting in a wealthy friend's home watching a video of his visit to Egypt. I was silently appalled at the sight of him walking through throngs of beggars, including blind children and child amputees, without offering them a penny.
>
> Many years later, I found myself lecturing in Egypt. Sure enough, as I left my hotel the first morning, I was surrounded by seemingly the same throng. As is my

---

of today's leading acting teachers, advises his students not to judge the characters whom they are playing; he regards this as one of the most common mistakes actors make. When an actor is asked to portray a character who has done evil things, Howard tells the actor that if he wishes to give a credible performance, he should not look at the character's behavior and say, "I would never do this." Rather, "The operative question for actors [should be] . . . 'What would make me do this? What would make me do what the character is doing?' " (see Howard Fine, *Fine on Acting: A Vision of the Craft*, pp. 89–95). In other words, instead of thinking, "Why would this character do such an awful thing?" the actor should ask himself, "What could I imagine happening to me that would cause me to do such a thing?"

custom at home, I was carrying dollar bills to give to the needy. As I began to dispense them, two things simultaneously occurred. First, the throng turned into a mob, a feeding frenzy with the amputees' crutches being used as weapons (a dollar is worth infinitely more there than at home), and second, my driver admonished me and warned me that I would regret my actions for the rest of my trip.

He was absolutely correct. I had been targeted. The throngs of beggars would follow me wherever I went. They would wait outside my hotel patiently, for hours if necessary, until I exited and then aggressively beseech me for the same ill-advised generosity that I had shown on the first day.

My wealthy friend was not being stingy; he was being wise.

The expression "to jump to a conclusion" almost always has a negative connotation. Few of us jump to positive assessments about others, but we are likely to seize upon a comment someone has made, an action someone has or has not taken, and assume a deficit in the person's character. When Hillel says, "Do not judge your fellow until you are in his place," he is merely asking that we extend to others the standard of judgment we want extended to ourselves. This brief teaching, only seven words in Hebrew (*al tadin et chaver'cha ad sheh'tagiya l'mkomo*) has the capacity to turn us into less angry, fairer and more loving people. Indeed, if this is the only one of Hillel's teachings recorded in this book that you incorporate into your life, you will still be profoundly transformed. Sometimes the greatest conversions take place inside the same religion.*

Intense Curiosity

He knew the speech of mountains, hills, and valleys.

—*Sofrim* 16:9

Hillel is most famous as a teacher, but the Talmud makes it clear that his ability to teach anyone was connected to his ability to learn from anyone. The knowledge attributed to him by the Talmud has a quasi-magical element, like the wisdom of Solomon, who, we are told, knew the language of the birds and the beasts. All creation was for Hillel a subject worthy of study and capable of imparting wisdom.

We already saw Hillel engaging in what, in Talmudic

---

* Judgmental people are apt to be highly conscious of the flaws of others, but not of their own (as a rule, we judge ourselves by our intentions and others by their actions). Hillel therefore urged people to guard against excessive self-confidence: "Do not be too sure of yourself until the day of your death" (*Ethics of the Fathers* 2:4). As the late British-Jewish scholar Hyam Maccoby commented: "This means that one should never think that one has overcome one's 'evil inclination,' for it is active in a human being as long as he has breath." This is perhaps the reason that Jewish tradition focuses little on birthdays (unlike the Western world, in which we honor famous people by commemorating their date of birth), but a great deal on the *yahrzeit*, the day of a person's death. Only when life is over can we fully assess whether it has been lived righteously and successfully.

times, constituted a type of scientific and anthropological speculation—why Babylonians' heads seemed to be rounder than those of other people and why Africans seemed to have wider feet. But Hillel's study of other cultures and of the natural world was far broader than this: "He even learned the languages of all the peoples of the world; as well as the speech of mountains, hills, and valleys, the speech of trees and grasses, the speech of wild and domestic animals, the speech of demons" (*Sofrim* 16:9). The sense that others come from traditions that might in themselves contain useful knowledge or information was clearly a key to Hillel's openness.

You Must Know Everything was the title of one of the last books by Isaac Babel, the renowned Soviet-Jewish writer. Such a designation might well apply to Hillel. Most people familiar with his name as a great rabbinic sage assume that his areas of expertise and of interest were confined to matters of Jewish concern.

How many languages did Hillel actually know? The Talmud cites only teachings of his in Hebrew and Aramaic (the language of his native Babylonia and probably the most widely spoken language in Israel at the time). For example, his summary of Judaism to the man standing on one foot was delivered in Aramaic. But this text from *Sofrim* indicates that he learned other languages as well. The word *prozbol*, the term that describes the famous legal formula by which Hillel avoided the wholesale cancellation of debts in the seventh year, is Greek (likely meaning "before the assembly of the councilors"; see p. 51), and so we can assume at least a basic mastery of Greek for Hillel to turn to that language for a word to explain his most far-reaching legal innovation. Indeed, while no other Talmudic sources refer to Hillel's using the Greek language, a passage in *Sotah* (49b) notes that his grandson, Rabbi Gamliel, who also headed the Sanhedrin, made sure that he and his household not only knew Greek, but were also familiar with Greek wisdom, more specifically, Greek philosophy.* Rabbi Gamliel's son, Rabbi Shimon, said that his father supported one thousand students, five hundred of whom devoted themselves to Torah studies, and five hundred to Greek wisdom. We do not know definitively of any other languages Hillel spoke, but it is likely that, as head of the Sanhedrin, he had some encounters with Roman officials and might therefore have acquired some knowledge of Latin (it is unlikely that Roman officials he met would have knowledge of Hebrew or Aramaic).

Behind the poetic manner in which the rabbis describe Hillel's far-reaching knowledge—"[he knew] the speech of mountains, hills, and valleys, the speech of trees and grasses, the speech of wild and domestic animals"—there is the real suggestion that he did study geography, botany, and zoology.

What is the connection between the well-known image of Hillel as Judaism's great ethical model and the largely overlooked sense of him as what might be called Judaism's first "renaissance man"? Clearly one link is an openness to the outside world, which takes courage as well as curiosity.

---

* I am grateful to Yitzhak Buxbaum for this reference (see Yitzhak Buxbaum, *The Life and Teachings of Hillel*, p. 224).

Everything, in this view, has been created by God and is therefore worthy of study, worthy of compassion. Which is why, in the Talmud, nothing botanical or zoological was alien to Hillel. But also why it would not be sufficient to say of Hillel that nothing Jewish was alien to him. Nothing *human* was alien to him, and this insight only served as a bulwark for his Jewish faith.

PART II

Hillel versus Shammai:
The Talmud's Most Famous
Adversaries

7

Hillel the Interpreter,
Shammai the Literalist

No discussion of Hillel is possible without an in-depth look at his great adversary, Shammai, whom we have already met chasing away an inquiring Gentile with a stick. Hillel and Shammai are not merely the Ali and Frazier of rabbinic Judaism; their interpretive styles—and disputations—lived on through their students and through the schools of thought they founded. At times, disputations between the School of Hillel and the School of Shammai grew so heated that the Talmud tells us of one tragic day when disciples of the School of Shammai attacked and, according to one text, killed disciples of the School of Hillel (Jerusalem Talmud, *Shabbat* 1:4).

In the ahistorical universe of the Talmud, followers argue down through the ages, the living argue with the dead, and followers may at times appear to precede those who influenced them. For this reason, along with the paucity of historical detail, this book is not strictly speaking a biography. It is, however, the biography more truly of an aspect of Judaism, one beautifully embodied by Hillel, who represents one of the many faces of Judaism—a face that I feel is too easily eclipsed.

It says something about Judaism that both Hillel and Shammai, and many of their followers, remain revered figures within traditional Judaism, even when they embody opposite approaches to the law and to life itself. In this regard, Talmudic Judaism is anti-fundamentalist. It isn't simply the answer that is prized, it is the argument itself, the culture of disputation, the wrestling with the truth.

Nevertheless, the differences in the approaches of these two great rabbis and of their schools of thought matter a great deal and are worth looking at in detail. The standard, oft-repeated impression of Shammai is of severity in demeanor and strictness in legal rulings (in the overwhelming majority of disputes between his disciples and those of Hillel, Shammai's school does in fact represent the stricter approach).

Even the few stories told about Shammai as a father and grandfather reveal more of a legalistic rather than paternal inclination. For example, he wanted his son, while still a child, to almost fully fast on Yom Kippur. In the words of the rabbis, he wished to feed him "with just one hand," until he was finally ordered to feed the boy more lavishly, "with both hands" (Tosefta *Yoma* 4:2).[1] When his daughter-in-law gave birth to a son on the holiday of Sukkot, Shammai broke off a part of the roof over the mother and child's bed and placed *s'chach* (the covering for a sukkah) over it so that this newborn could observe in some fashion the mitzvah of being in a sukkah (Mishnah *Sukkah* 2:8).

Some of this of course may be merely a difference of temperament. If life is an anxious business, fulfillment of the law will be an anxious business, and a request for extreme brevity from a Gentile would be an occasion for rage and resentment. But there is also an authentic religious difference between Hillel's and Shammai's views of the law.

A good place to begin examining the differences between the House of Hillel and the House of Shammai, before circling back to their emblematic difference of opinion over the welcoming of converts, is with a dispute over the Shema.

The Shema ("Hear O Israel, the Lord is our God, the Lord is One") is Judaism's most important statement of faith and its most famous prayer. When recited in the prayer service, it is followed by three paragraphs, the first of which (the *ve-ahavta*; Deut. 6:4–9) contains mention of many of Judaism's most basic laws. In this paragraph, Jews are commanded, "And you shall love the Lord your God with all your heart, with all your soul, and with all your might." That is one of the Torah's 613 commandments. The laws of tefillin and mezuzah are set forth here as well. And yet another verse enjoins us to "take to heart these instructions with which I charge you this day. Teach them to your children. Speak of them when you are at home and when you are on the road, when you lie down and when you rise up."

These last words serve as the basis for the law requiring Jews to recite the Shema twice daily. But when and how must they do so? The answer hinges on how one understands the words "when you lie down and when you rise up." The School of Shammai taught, "In the evening, everyone should lie down in order to recite [the Shema], and in the morning [each person] must stand, for it is written, 'when you lie down and when you rise up.' " But the School of Hillel taught: "Each person recites the Shema according to his preferred manner [that is, one can do so while sitting or standing, while lying down or walking]."

The Mishnah, in which this dispute is recorded (*Berakhot* 1:3), asks how the Hillelites explained the Torah's words "when you lie down and when you rise up," and answers that they believed that the words were not meant to be understood literally. Rather, the Torah's intention was to establish the proper time to recite the Shema, once in the evening, the hours when people lie down for the night, and once in the morning, when they arise.

Rabbi Tarfon, who lived a century after Hillel and Shammai, was more impressed with the School of Shammai's reasoning (in general, he inclined toward Shammai's positions). The Mishnah records his autobiographical recollection: "I was walking on the road and when the time arrived for the evening Shema, I lay down to recite it in accordance with the views of the House of Shammai, and I thereby endangered myself because of the bandits who might have attacked me while I was lying on the road" (Mishnah *Berakhot* 1:3).

At this point in time, the rabbis had already established that the rulings of Hillel and his disciples were the accepted Jewish practice, and Rabbi Tarfon's colleagues were vexed by his behavior. They said to him: "You yourself are responsible for what might have happened to you, for [by deliberately lying down for the Shema] you violated the words of the School of Hillel."

This passage, only the third ruling in the first of the Mishnah's sixty-three books, foreshadows a common theme in the disputes between Hillel and his disciples and Shammai and his. Shammai's innate, though not exclusive, tendency was to understand Torah law literally. Therefore, if the Torah says that the words are to be recited "when you lie down," one must lie down to say this prayer. Hillel's approach was geared more toward addressing the question, "What is it that the Bible wishes to communicate in this verse?" And the answer his followers came to, at least as I understand it, is that the Torah is instructing us to focus our attention on God and His commandments at least twice every day, once in the evening and once in the morning. What matters, therefore, is not our physical posture while doing so, but that we concentrate our minds and recite the prayer during the appropriate time periods.

How do we explain, therefore, Rabbi Tarfon's inclination to defer to the rejected opinion of the School of Shammai? The answer probably has much to do with Rabbi Tarfon's own literalist inclinations. There are a series of questions and answers recorded at the beginning of the fourth chapter of the Mishnaic book *Pirkei Avot (Ethics of the Fathers)*, the most famous of which is "Who is rich?" to which Ben Zoma answers, "One who is happy with what he has." From Ben Zoma's perspective, a person who has a great deal of money but is always worried that he does not have enough, or that he might lose what he has, cannot be classified as rich, because one of the presumed benefits of wealth is that you do not have to worry about money. Conversely, a person with little money who appreciates what he does have—instead of worrying about what he doesn't—can be classified as wealthy.

This teaching, with its unique, unexpected definition of wealth, is among the best-known of all rabbinic aphorisms. Relatively few people know, however, that the same question was answered quite differently by Rabbi Tarfon. His response as to who is rich was, "One who has a hundred vineyards and a hundred fields and a hundred servants to work them" (*Shabbat* 25b).

Is it any surprise that a man who offers so straightforward and literal a response to such a question would also feel constrained to lie down at night in the middle of a road so as to satisfy the Torah's command, "when you lie down"?

In arguing that Hillel and his disciples are interpreters and Shammai and his followers literalists (of course, this refers to general trends and not to every position they take), one might counter that even a literal reading of something may be an interpretation of it. What truly distinguishes the different approaches, and what may be a better term, is the metaphorical impulse behind the readings of the School of Hillel. "Moral imagination" is one of the traits we attributed to Hillel in the last chapter. Here the emphasis falls on imagination itself.*

---

* As an alternative to the interpretation offered here, Professor Michael Berger of Emory University argues that "when you lie down and when you rise up" is not necessarily being read by Hillelites metaphorically, but as a literal reference to a time period. The Hebrew, as Professor Berger understands it, can be seen as ambiguous, either referring to posture (as Shammaites understand it) or time (as Hillelites understand it).

The fact that Rabbi Tarfon offers up his understanding of how to carry out this commandment by telling this story ("I lay down in the road") immediately suggests the limitations of so literalist an approach. One has only to picture the man lying in a road frequented by bandits to realize he's suffering from a dangerous lack of imagination. The Talmud does not merely say that he is wrong, it embodies the need for imagination by its very methods.

The notion that we sometimes need to read even the words of the Torah with an eye to the metaphorical is a great element of rabbinic Judaism, but surely was also an anxiety-provoking one for a group of men trying to hold a culture and a religion together. All the rabbis had to counter the dominance of the Roman Empire was the authority of the Torah and the force of their words. Imagination was needed, but there was always the anxiety that imagination would cross the line, exceed its authority, depart too fully from the literal, and end—as Christianity did—not merely reinterpreting the Hebrew Bible but metaphorizing it out of literal existence and turning it into the foundation of a new faith altogether.

This balancing act, between law and story, between legalistic literalism and imaginative freedom, is necessary to keep in mind when thinking about the disputations between the schools of Hillel and Shammai, and also when thinking about Judaism today. Our personal freedoms have never been greater but, in our post-Holocaust, assimilating world, anxiety about continuity has never been higher.

8

Thieves, Brides, and When Lying Is a Virtue

The tension between the literal and the metaphorical interpretations of Jewish law is evident in several other disputes among Hillel's and Shammai's disciples and are worth looking at. For example, the Talmud asks, what should be the obligation of a thief who wishes to repent? The most obvious first demand is that he return to his victim the object he has stolen; indeed, this is what the Torah commands: "[and he] shall restore that which he took by robbery" (Lev. 5:23).

But then the Talmud asks: What if he stole a beam of wood and used it in the construction of a house? To the literalists of the School of Shammai, the answer is clear: "He must demolish the whole [building] and restore the beam to its owner" (*Gittin* 55a). To Hillel's disciples, the answer is equally clear: he must restore to the owner the monetary value of the stolen beam.

Again, the rabbis ruled in favor of the Hillelites, concluding that the School of Shammai's ruling would impose so great a hardship on the thief (forcing him to tear down his house) that he would decide never to repent. As Rashi

(1040–1105), the foremost commentator on both the Torah and Talmud, expressed it: "For if you force him to destroy his dwelling and return the beam to its owner, he will avoid the act of repentance" (commentary on *Gittin* 55a). Here, Shammai's literalism would lead to two unhappy results: the thief likely won't repent and his victim, therefore, won't be compensated.

This literalist tendency ends up making little sense. Is it logical to assume that the victim of the theft has so deep an attachment to the stolen beam that he will be satisfied with nothing less than its physical return? I suspect that any such victim would be motivated more by a spirit of revenge (the desire to force the thief to tear down his dwelling) than by any sentimental attachment to the beam. Ironically, letting the victim indulge his desire for his specific beam might well put the person in violation of a Torah commandment, "Do not take revenge or bear a grudge against members of your people" (Lev. 19:18). Vengeance is specifically prohibited by the Torah, yet why else would the victim insist on the return of this specific beam?[1]

In general, the question of what the Torah wants is one that particularly animated Hillel (see the discussion of the *prozbol* on pp. 51–52). For Shammai and his disciples the question of what the Torah wants does not generally require a delving into the Torah's motives. What the Torah wants is precisely what it says:* it wants people to lie down when

---

* Perhaps the most famous rabbinic supporter of Shammai's approach was Rabbi Eliezer ben Hyrcanus, regarded as the greatest scholar of his age (though many of his rulings were rejected). Rabbi Eliezer, alone among the sages, argued that the verse "an eye for an eye" (Exod. 21:24) should be

they recite the Shema, and thieves to restore precisely that which they have stolen, whether or not such a demand causes fewer thieves to repent and fewer victims to be compensated.

In a certain sense, the literalist approach is easier to follow because it can free a person from struggling with issues of intention. But this approach also can lead to suffering for those subjected to it, as yet a third dispute between the schools of Hillel and Shammai reveals.

In this instance, the focus of the discussion is proper etiquette at a wedding:

Our rabbis taught: "How does one dance [and what words does one say] before a bride?" The School of Shammai says, "The bride [is described] as she is." The School of Hillel says, "[Every bride is described as] a beautiful and graceful bride."

The School of Shammai said to the School of Hillel, "If she is lame or blind, does one say of her, 'Beautiful and graceful bride'? Does not the Torah command, 'Stay far away from falsehood?'"

But the School of Hillel answered the School of Shammai, "According to your words, if a person has made a bad purchase in the marketplace, should one praise it to him or deprecate it? Surely one should praise it to him."*

---

interpreted literally (see *Bava Kamma* 83b–84a), a point of view the Talmud uniformly rejects. According to the rabbis, one who puts out the eye of another is required to pay financial damages as determined by the courts, but physical retribution is outlawed.

* It is interesting that the School of Shammai seems to take no issue with

Therefore, the rabbis teach, "One's disposition should always be pleasant with people.' " (*Ketubot* 16b–17a)[2]

Though the practice of lying about the quality of a purchase may indeed be—at least sometimes—questionable, the notion that one's disposition should be pleasant certainly accords with Hillel's treatment of the Gentile seeking conversion. More than that, Hillel treats the Gentile not as he is but as he wishes he were or might become. And in a sort of magical optimism familiar to many Americans—by believing in the American dream it often comes true—the Gentile indeed becomes a devoted Jew, as do the others seeking conversion who are treated not as they present themselves but as they might become.

The crux of the Hillel/Shammai debate over the praising of a bride hinges on whether or not the Torah verse "Stay far away from falsehood" (Exod. 23:7) should always be understood literally. In fact, the wording of the verse seems so straightforward that it would seem that Shammai, on this occasion, must be more in the right than Hillel. But even in this case, Hillel's disciples argue that truth, in and of itself, is not an absolute value.

Or is it?

Throughout history, the absolutist position suggested in this debate—that truth is always paramount—has also been expressed (in terms more extreme than anything intended

---

this rhetorical question, though it is by no means self-evident (at least to me) that the Shammaites would sanction lying to someone who made a bad purchase and asked our opinion.

by the School of Shammai) by religious and secular figures in other traditions. Saint Augustine, perhaps the most influential of the Church Fathers, argued that lying, even when doing so could save another's life, was both unjustifiable and foolish: "Does he not speak most perversely who says that one person ought to die spiritually, so another may live? . . . Since, then, eternal life is lost by lying, a lie may never be told for the preservation of the temporal life of another" ("On Lying," in *Treatises on Various Subjects*).

Catholic theology holds, therefore, that lying is always wrong. John Henry Cardinal Newman, one of the nineteenth century's foremost Catholic theologians, argued against lying even more forcefully than did Augustine: "The Catholic Church holds it better for the sun and moon to drop from heaven, for the earth to fail, and for all the many millions who are upon it to die of starvation in extremist agony . . . than that one soul . . . should commit one venial sin, should tell one willful untruth, though it harmed no one."

Immanuel Kant (1724–1804), the most influential secular moral philosopher of the modern world (Kant believed in God but excluded religious arguments from his philosophy), likewise argued that lying is always wrong. In his essay "On a Supposed Right to Lie from Benevolent Motives," he stated that if a would-be murderer inquires "whether our friend who is pursued by him has taken refuge in our home," we are forbidden to lie to him.

As I read these positions, I wonder if those pursued by murderers—as millions of people were in Germany* in the

* Kant's homeland, and the country in which he exerted his greatest influence.

1930s and 1940s—would have thought it wrong to lie to them, or whether the millions of people who died of starvation during the nineteenth century in which Cardinal Newman lived would have denounced as immoral those who lied so that they and their children might eat. And perhaps, throughout history, brides might not have appreciated as moral heroes those who come to their weddings and who describe them as they are, warts and all.[3]

Whether or not a person is cruel by inclination, an attachment to literalism can lead one to advocate cruel behavior. Hillel's and his disciples' view of truth was a more instrumental one. Of course, being truthful is important, and the biblical verse, "Stay far away from falsehood" almost always—but not uniformly—applies. But sometimes, other values, such as saving lives and not hurting people, override it.[4]

Fifteen hundred years after Hillel and Shammai, the *Shulchan Arukh*, Rabbi Joseph Caro's great sixteenth-century code of Jewish law, ruled, "It is a mitzvah [commandment] to gladden the bridegroom and the bride and to dance before them and to say that she is beautiful and graceful, even if she is not" (*Even Ha-Ezer* 65:1).

The essence of Hillel is embodied in that ruling. His feelings about how one greets a Jewish bride have endured within Judaism far better than his feelings about how one greets a Gentile seeking conversion, or his establishment of ethics as the bedrock demand of Jewish religiosity. Certainly there are many reasons for this, from the rampant assimilation following the Enlightenment to the treatment of Jews by Gentiles in the two thousand years since Hillel lived—

treatment that has often accounted for the wariness and wrath of Shammai. But the time now seems ripe to ask whether American Jews of the twenty-first century might show the same openness, courage, and imagination that Hillel displayed in the first century.

9

Issues Regarding Women

Having argued against the literalism of Shammai, I need to add that although Hillel's victories can look easy and obvious, Shammai and his school should not be mistaken for the Talmudic equivalent of the Washington Generals playing the Harlem Globetrotters—merely as foils to be defeated.

Both sages play for the same team; the battles between Hillel and Shammai should be seen as signs of health within the religion, for they are fights about alternate interpretive pathways to the same God. It is balance that matters to the health of a religion, and just as it is basic to the health of a democracy that there be opposition parties, so, too, is it basic to a religion's moral and nontotalitarian underpinnings that there be critics of the status quo and alternative views and emphases.

One of the glories of the polyphonic lessons of the Talmud is that the literalism of Shammai can at times turn out to be the more liberal path. Looking at legal issues involving women is a good place to discover this. From previous chapters, you might assume that Hillel's views regarding women would be more expansive than those of Shammai. But, you'd be wrong.

In a notable legal disputation about divorce, the School of Hillel takes a more conservative, patriarchal (one might argue, regressive) stance on the status of women than does the School of Shammai. The fundamental argument between the two schools on the legal grounds necessary for a man to divorce his wife hinges on how literally one interprets a biblical verse, "A man takes a wife. . . . She fails to find favor in his eyes because he finds *something unseemly* about her and he writes her a bill of divorce . . ." (Deut. 24:1; emphasis added).

In this instance, Shammai's literalism inclines him to a view more protective of women. According to Shammai, *ervat davar*, the words translated as "something unseemly," connote a forbidden sexual act. The School of Shammai, therefore, rules that the sole justification for divorcing one's wife is sexual impropriety—most commonly, adultery. The School of Hillel chooses to interpret "something unseemly" as meaning "for any reason at all," including, to cite the example the Hillelites offer, a man's anger at his wife for spoiling his meal. A century after Hillel, Rabbi Akiva, the leading rabbi of his age and a man who stood firmly in the traditions of Hillel, argued that a man could divorce his wife if he found another woman whom he regarded as more attractive (see *Gittin* 9:10; Rabbi Akiva roots his position in the verse's earlier words, "she fails to find favor in his eyes").*

---

* These differing positions of the two schools might help explain the rationale behind the debate on how to praise a bride (see pp. 92–93). Hillel ruled that at weddings all brides should be described as "beautiful and virtuous."

Another dispute between the schools concerned women's testimony. Jewish courts generally rejected testimony offered by women on the grounds that the Torah did not consider them to be valid witnesses. But if a woman testified that her husband had died and that she should therefore be permitted to remarry, the Shammaites accepted her testimony as valid. The School of Hillel accepted her testimony only if there were other witnesses to the fact of her husband's death who could be summoned if necessary; only then, they felt, could it be assumed that the woman would be afraid to lie, and her testimony, therefore, could be regarded as trustworthy.

Since the School of Shammai accepted the woman's testimony in such cases, it also permitted her to collect the money payable to widows according to the marriage contract (the *ketubah*). The School of Hillel, because it did not generally accept her testimony as valid, did not allow her to collect this large lump sum, but, instead, restricted her to a budget taken from the estate to pay for her expenses.

The Mishnah records that in both these instances, the School of Hillel ultimately retracted its view and accepted

Given that Hillel granted a man the right to divorce his wife for any reason whatsoever, it makes sense that he would encourage all wedding participants to engage in great—and perhaps inaccurate and untruthful—praise of the bride; the consequences to the wife of the husband becoming displeased with her were so severe that it made sense for the Hillelites to insist that the husband hear only great praise of his wife's beauty. But the School of Shammai saw no pressing reason to compromise on the biblical law to "stay far away from falsehood," because even if the husband concluded that his wife was not attractive—and realized that others also thought so—there was nothing he could do about it. Divorce was not an option, unless the woman committed adultery.

the ruling of the School of Shammai (Mishnah *Yevamot* 15:2–3). We are, after all, shaped by our adversaries. Hillel, and the School of Hillel, needed Shammai and his followers, in most instances to define their own positions against, but also at times to absorb into, their own positions.

On yet another issue, the School of Hillel's ruling comes across as more appreciative of women than that of Shammai. The first of the Torah's 613 laws is "Be fruitful and multiply" (Gen. 1:28). But how many children must a couple have to properly fulfill this commandment? The School of Hillel rules that having two children, one of each sex, is sufficient (based on Gen. 5:2),* since by doing so, the couple will have replaced themselves. The School of Shammai rules that the couple must have at least two sons; it offers no ruling concerning daughters (Mishnah *Yevamot* 6:6).

It would seem to me that the School of Shammai's ruling must have caused great pain to families to whom only daughters were born, and who were made to feel that the birth had no religious significance.

The Talmud, generally thin on biographical detail, does give us a glimpse into Hillel's personal life—though only a glimpse. And just as it is unsurprising to find Shammai feeding his son on Yom Kippur "with one hand," so it is perhaps unsurprising to find in the story of Hillel and his

---

* Most observant couples, in any case, have more than two children, but two is understood as constituting the minimum to fulfill the commandment.

wife a tale of generosity and abundance. We know little about Hillel's relationship with his wife—one story, to be precise (we have no stories concerning Shammai and his wife)—but the story casts him in a loving light and represents his wife as embodying his own devotion to strangers and to charity.

On one occasion, we learn, Hillel arranged for a friend to dine with him, but at just the moment dinner was to be served, a poor, hungry man came to the door, where he was greeted by Hillel's wife (whose name, unhappily, is unknown to us). The fellow told her that he was to be married that day and had no food for himself and his soon-to-be bride. Taking pity on the man, she gave him all the food she had prepared, and then cooked a new meal, a painstaking and cumbersome process. For reasons unexplained in the story, she didn't inform her husband that the meal would be delayed, and only when it was ready did she emerge from the kitchen. Hillel said to her, "My dear, why did you not bring the food sooner?" She told him what had happened, and Hillel said, "I really did not judge you critically, but meritoriously, because everything you did was for the glory of God's Name" (*Derekh Eretz Rabbah*, 6:2).

Ethical behavior, in this story, trumps abstract expectations about the duties of a wife. Certainly the mood of the story is far from the ruling about the right to divorce a woman who displeases her husband by the way she prepares a meal.

But this sweet account of Hillel's high regard for his wife's character is not exactly proto-feminist. The Oral Law was, in Hillel's day, still oral—not written down as it later was in the Talmud—and therefore it retained greater flexibility, enabling it to mediate more easily between shifting contemporary circumstances and abiding religious principles. After the cataclysmic events in the two centuries following Hillel's death, particularly the destruction of the Temple and the two failed revolts against Rome (66–70 C.E. and 132–135 C.E.), the law, though still debated and argued, lost an element of its flexible character as it became codified. This codification, in turn, led to even less flexibility in the interpretation of the Oral Law.*

In Hillel's time, the Gentile seeking instruction was a troubling source of disputation between battling schools of rabbinic thought. In modern times, women pursuing advanced religious study have often been in the role of the stranger, even when they come from inside the Jewish world. Applying Talmudic lessons to the twenty-first century determined by an almost entirely male world two thousand years ago in itself requires an act of imaginative interpretation of just the sort that Hillel himself so often employed.

* This point is developed in Eliezer Berkovits's analysis of the development of Jewish law, *Not in Heaven*.

10

Shammai Beyond Stereotype

Isaac Bashevis Singer, the late Nobel Prize–winning writer, liked to say that an important feature of good characterization in a novel is that the characters are dimensionalized and are not all of one piece. Human beings, as Singer noted, have contradictions. For example, compassionate people will sometimes reveal a toughness that we would not have anticipated, while stern people often show surprising softer aspects to their personalities. Such, I would argue, is the case with Shammai.

Unlike Hillel, whose aphorisms are quoted extensively in *Ethics of the Fathers*, we have only a few teachings of Shammai, the best-known of which is "Receive every person with a cheerful expression" (*Ethics of the Fathers* 1:15). On the one hand, there is something almost humorous in hearing this suggestion proffered by the man who chased away two questioners with a stick and a third with an insult. On the other hand, this statement might well reflect a particularly impressive aspect of Shammai: he knew himself, including his weaknesses. Unlike Hillel, to whom calmness and pleasantness, it seems, came more naturally and without the need for reminders, Shammai knew he had an irascible nature and, to his credit, formulated this teaching to remind himself to behave amicably. To this day, I remain impressed by people who know their weaknesses and formulate strategies to guard against them.

Another statement quoted in Shammai's name in *Ethics of the Fathers* conveys balanced and highly sensible advice: "Say little and do much." In other words, don't promise to do a lot for others; among other things, such promises excite expectations and often lead to disappointment. Rather, promise only a little, and then let your deeds exceed your words.

Such behavior is associated with the patriarch Abraham, who invites three travelers in the desert to dine with him in his tent. In extending his invitation, Abraham minimizes what he will do for his guests; he will "fetch a morsel of bread that you may refresh yourselves" (Gen. 18:5).* But he then serves an elaborate meal, complete with a young calf and cake. The Talmud sees Abraham's behavior as emblematic of a righteous person, in contrast to that of Ephron of Hebron, who offers Abraham a gift of land on which to bury Sarah, who has just died (Gen. 23:11). But when Abraham insists on paying for the land, Ephron charges him a very high price,[1] leading us to think that his initial offer of a gift was merely empty words. In the words of a later Talmudic passage, echoing Shammai's dictum, "The righteous (tzad-

---

* Promising little also makes invitees less embarrassed to accept an invitation, as little hardship will be imposed on the host.

dikim) say little and do much, while the wicked say much
and do not even do a little" (*Bava Metzia* 87a).

Shammai's third teaching in *Ethics of the Fathers* is a practical dictum on study: "Make your study of Torah a fixed
activity." In other words, learn daily and set aside a fixed
amount of time for study. From such fixed activities, great
accomplishments will ensue, which would not be the case if
one's learning is spontaneous and unscheduled.

While Shammai's reputation was one of stubbornness (we
have instances of Hillel and his disciples retracting their
positions in favor of Shammai, but we have at most one
example of the reverse (see p. 229, fn.); one Talmudic tale
shows Shammai as willing to concede, though grudgingly,
the validity of another's logic.

A man had sons who, in the words of the Talmud, "were
not conducting themselves properly." In consequence, the
man bequeathed his entire estate to Yonatan ben Uzziel, Hillel's foremost disciple. Yonatan divided the estate in three
parts; one third he set aside for his own needs, one third he
consecrated to the Temple, and one third he gave to the dead
man's sons. Shammai heard about Yonatan's ruling and was
outraged. He went to Yonatan and rebuked him for violating
the deceased's wishes: "The man wished to leave nothing
to these sons, and you gave them back a third." Yonatan
replied: "Shammai, if you can find legal grounds for nullify-
ing the third that I took for myself, and the third that I consecrated, then you can also nullify what I gave as a gift to the
sons. If you cannot, then acknowledge that this is my property to sell or to sanctify, and it is also mine to give as a gift."

In other words, once the man bequeathed the estate to Yonatan with no strings attached, it was Yonatan's to do with as he wished.[2]

Shammai had no answer to Yonatan's argument, but also seems to have felt that the young sage had not addressed him with proper deference (perhaps Shammai didn't like that Yonatan called him by his first name): "The son of Uzziel cast abuse on me," was all Shammai would say, acknowledging by implication that Yonatan's reasoning was irrefutable (*Bava Batra* 133b–134a).

Yonatan's behavior was in keeping with the ethos of Hillel, who, in his behavior toward those impertinent seekers of conversion, bestowed gifts on them that they had not yet earned but that he hoped they would become worthy of. Lurking behind these seemingly localized arguments is a larger principle of transmission: How does one pass material on from one generation to the next; who is qualified to receive it, and on what grounds?

Yonatan, in line with a ruling in the Mishnah, knew that a man has the right to disinherit his children, but he also felt, as does the Mishnah, that it is wrong to avail oneself of this right (see *Mishnah Bava Batra* 8:5). Therefore, like Hillel in the case of the *prozbol*, he found a legal way to circumvent a law whose enforcement, he thought, would lead to inequity.

There is a ruling by Shammai, which is infrequently cited, that seems to me to represent a more equitable solution than the more generally accepted view offered in the Talmud. The rabbis are discussing an instance in which a man has hired another to commit a seriously forbidden act, such as murder, and the hired man does so. Who is guilty in such a case? The dominant view in the Talmud is that legal responsibility lies *exclusively* with the one who carried out the deed, not with the one who hired him.

The Talmud explains this ruling with the statement, "There is no [such thing as a] messenger in a case of sin" (*Kiddushin* 42b). Normally, a messenger is not held responsible for his actions as a messenger, no matter how distasteful; instead, all blame is directed at the message's sender. That is because a messenger is not regarded as an independent agent but merely as the representative of the one who sent him. But if a messenger is sent to perform an illegal act, he cannot defend himself by saying that he was acting only as someone's agent. Because "there is no messenger in a case of sin," he bears full and personal responsibility for any evil he does. Human beings are obligated to obey God's laws, and it is the responsibility of one who is instructed or offered a bribe to do an illegal act to refuse to do so because it contravenes God's will. If the person does commit the act, he cannot blame the one who commanded him. As the Talmud asks, rhetorically, "If the words of the teacher [in this case, meaning God] and the words of the student [in this case, the man who is sending one to sin] conflict, whose words should you obey?"

But Shammai opposed this ruling, arguing that a person who orders or hires another to do an illegal act bears primary responsibility. His prooftext is the biblical narrative that recounts the story of King David's brief, forbidden relationship with Bathsheba, the wife of Uriah, an officer in

David's army (see 2 Sam. 11:2–5). When Bathsheba reveals to David that she is pregnant, he summons Uriah to the palace, hoping that while in Jerusalem, Uriah will go home, sleep with his wife, and then, when a child is born seven months later, assume that it is a premature birth and that the child is his. But Uriah refuses to enjoy himself with his wife while his comrades are in battle,[3] and David, fearing a scandal, sends a sealed letter to Joab, his army commander, ordering him to have Uriah killed in battle: "Set Uriah in the forefront of the hottest battle and withdraw from him, so that he may be hit and die" (11:15). Joab does so.

According to the reasoning of the Talmudic rabbis, Joab should bear the responsibility for Uriah's death, as he is the one who sends Uriah to his death. But, Shammai notes, it is David, not Joab, whom the prophet Nathan denounces for Uriah's death (2 Sam. 12:1–10). In Shammai's view, Nathan's moral standard, that the one who orders another to kill someone (or, as in this case, to have someone killed) is the one who bears primary guilt. Of course, Joab shouldn't have obeyed David's order, but if not for that order, Joab would not have harmed Uriah. So why excuse from responsibility the person ordering, or soliciting the act?

Here, it is Shammai who is unwilling to follow the precise letter of Jewish law as it is understood by most of the rabbis[4] (that only the one who carried out the forbidden act bears criminal guilt, not the one who ordered it), and it is his ruling that strikes me as more just.

In actuality, of course, there is grave guilt on both sides. That is why most people reject the common defense offered by war criminals, "I was only following orders," and want to see these people punished. But they also want to see the officials who issued the immoral orders punished; in truth, most people see these officials as bearing even greater guilt, an attitude that corresponds to the position taken by Shammai.*

Although we have already discussed the way in which the Shammaites' interpretation of the injunction to be fruitful and multiply led them to ordain a preferred sex for one's offspring, the same principle led them in another case to a ruling that seems to hold out more humanity than Hillel's. The case occurs in the Mishnaic tractate *Gittin* and involves an instance that must have been rare even at the time of the Talmud:

> One who is half-slave and half-free [perhaps, Rashi conjectures, the slave was owned by two brothers who had inherited him from their father, and one of them had emancipated him] works one day for his master and one day for himself. These are the words of the School of Hillel. But the School of Shammai says: "You have benefited the master, but not the slave. For it is impossible for him to marry a slave woman, because half of him is already a free man, and it is impossible for him to marry a free woman because half of him is still a slave [such marriages were forbidden]. Shall he there-

---

* I think an innate sense of justice in most people assigns greater guilt to one who carries out an evil act for money than to one who does so when ordered by a superior in a position of authority. Thus, it is more difficult for a soldier to refuse a commanding officer's order, even when immoral and illegal, than for a civilian to refuse a monetary offer to commit a crime.

fore never marry? But was not the world created only so that people be fruitful and increase, as it is written, 'He [God] did not create the world to be desolate, He formed it to be inhabited' (Isa. 45:18). Rather, because of *tikkun olam* we force his master to free him, and the slave writes a note obliging him to pay off the master for half his value. And the School of Hillel reversed itself to rule in accordance with the School of Shammai. (Mishnah *Gittin* 4:5)

Several things are striking in this ruling. First, the School of Shammai's concern for the well-being of the slave shows a more humanitarian inclination in this case than that shown by the School of Hillel. Second, the Shammaites root their legal ruling in *tikkun olam*, a category until now associated with Hillel's legislative enactments (see chapter 5). Finally, the willingness of the Hillelites to change their ruling reminds us that at its best, the disputations between the two schools served as a system of mutual transformation. The Shammaites reached a humane solution on the basis of *tikkun olam*, the very principle their opponent Hillel had pioneered. The Hillelites, in turn, were persuaded by their own logic, filtered through the minds of their adversaries.

The stereotypical image of Shammai—severe, humorless, stubborn, and obsessed with the letter of the law—tells a truth about him, but not a complete one. This man, whose disciples were concerned that the law not be interpreted as forbidding a slave from marrying and having a family or permitting a man to cast off his wife simply because he was displeased with her (see p. 98), had softer edges to him as well. It was perhaps his misfortune in life (and even more so in history) to be a foil for Hillel, the preeminent exemplar of halakhic humanism. Always being judged in comparison with Hillel could do damage to anyone's good name. Which is why, perhaps, we find to this day many institutions and Jewish children named for Hillel, but I cannot think of a single institution named for Shammai.

11

Two Torahs: Deciding Between Hillel and Shammai

The Talmud records only three actual disputes between Hillel and Shammai, and the issues involved, dealing with menstruating women, the dough offering, and the waters of the *mikvah*, or ritual bath, are quite technical in nature (Mishnah *Eduyot* 1:1–3).¹

And whose view triumphs in these disputes? Ironically, neither.

But in the decades following Hillel's and Shammai's deaths, the disputes between their followers grew exponentially. In the Talmud's words, "When the disciples of Shammai and Hillel who had insufficiently studied with them increased in number, disputes proliferated in Israel and the Torah became as two Torahs" (*Sanhedrin* 88b).

Eventually, the legal disputes separating the schools expanded to 316. Talmud scholar Shmuel Safrai notes that there were large areas of Jewish law in which there was little disagreement between the two schools, including the laws concerning sacrifices, priestly service, the Sanhedrin, and the death penalty. But a plethora of disputes existed on issues involving prayers and blessings (see, for example, the differing views on how to understand the words from the Shema "when you lie down and when you rise up"; pp. 85–86), agricultural regulations, Shabbat and holiday rituals, laws of purity, and laws concerning divorce (see p. 98).[2] It is from the general thrust of the rulings on these issues that Shammai and the school named for him acquired the reputation for being stricter than Hillel and the School of Hillel. By and large, the reputation was deserved. For example, the School of Hillel declared an old sukkah valid for use, while the School of Shammai forbade it (Mishnah *Sukkah* 1:1). The School of Shammai forbade soaking [the ingredients of] ink and dry-stuffs on Friday unless there was time for them to be fully soaked before sundown, but the School of Hillel permitted it (Mishnah *Shabbat* 1:5).

On the other hand, there is a tradition attributed to Rabbi Meir that there are twenty-four cases, and some argue more than twice as many, in which the rulings of the Shammaites are more lenient (see Jerusalem Talmud, *Beitzah* 1:3). One reason for the disagreements on the precise number of leniencies is that it is not always clear what constitutes strictness and what constitutes leniency. For example, in a society in which the right of divorce is vested solely in the hands of the husband, does permitting a husband to divorce a wife for any reason whatsoever, as does Hillel (Mishnah *Gittin* 9:10), reflect a lenient ruling of Hillel's (it makes life easier for the dissatisfied husband)? Or is Shammai's ruling, which allows divorce only for reasons of sexual impropriety, and therefore offers greater protection to the wife, the lenient one (see p. 98)?*

Some disputes between the two schools involve issues that seem arcane and technical, and most modern readers would find it hard to imagine these disputes evoking great passion and controversy. Professor Safrai discusses one such dispute: "According to the *halacha*, food does not become susceptible to defilement (*tumah*) unless it comes in contact with water. The expressions in Leviticus 11:34–38, 'all meat . . . on which water comes' and 'if water be put upon the seed' were interpreted to mean that only if water was put on the food and that by a willful [human] act and not by itself (rain, irrigation, etc.), does the food become susceptible to defilement by a source of impurity. The dispute between the two schools hinges on the status of, for example, fruit which was sprinkled with water by a willful act not intended to sprinkle that fruit—such as if one shakes water off a bundle of herbs—and it touches the fruit nearby. In such cases, the Shammaites declare that fruit susceptible, because the water reached it through a purposeful act. The Hillelites, however, extend the concept of intention to include not only the water but the fruit as well. The one who shook the bundle of herbs had no interest in the water

---

* Obviously, in a society in which divorce proceedings can be initiated by either party, permitting a divorce for any reason would constitute the lenient position.

touching the fruit, and thus it is declared not susceptible to impurity."³*

But a few of the schools' disputes cover broad philosophical themes, none more so than the debate in *Eruvin* 13b, on whether it would have been better from humankind's perspective for human beings never to have been created. The Hillelites, in line with their founder's fundamentally optimistic nature (see pp. 68–70), espoused the view that it is better for people to have been created, while the Shammaites argued the opposite. What *is* surprising is that when a vote was finally taken to resolve this issue, some of the Hillelites seem to have defected to the Shammaite position; thus, the majority of the sages concluded: "It is better for man not to have been created." But unwilling to end so momentous a debate with so demoralizing a conclusion, the rabbis append, "But now that he has been created, let him examine his deeds." In other words, arguing about whether or not it is better to have been created is ultimately a moot issue. All we can do is respond to the reality of our existence with righteous deeds, along the lines of the concluding verse of the generally pessimistic book of Ecclesiastes: "The end of the matter, when all is said and done: revere God and observe His commandments, for that is all of man" (Eccles. 12:13).

Yet another philosophical and speculative debate between the schools centers on the question of the order of God's

---

* In line with contemporary anthropological writings, Rabbi Irwin Kula notes that issues of purity and impurity, and of intention, are ways in which the rabbis maintained order in the face of disorder, randomness, and chaos.

creation. The School of Shammai insisted that the creation of heaven preceded that of earth, while the School of Hillel argued the reverse (*Genesis Rabbah* 1:15). According to Hillel, the earth, where humankind dwells, was created first, a viewpoint that underscores man's centrality.[4] Certainly it is of a piece with the religious humanism of Hillel's response to the Gentile seeking conversion. He doesn't start by speaking to the man about God, but instead tells him not to do to others what is hateful to him. Is this not to say, in a sense, that the earth comes first?

The struggles between the two schools generally were civil. For instance, the Talmud records that despite differing views on marriage laws, the Shammaites did not refrain from marrying women of the School of Hillel, nor did the Hillelites refrain from marrying women of the School of Shammai. Rather, they treated each other "with affection and friendship" (*Yevamot* 14b says that they would inform one another of relationships that the other side would regard as problematic).* Similarly, a Mishnah in *Ethics of the Fathers* offers Hillel and Shammai as model intellectual combatants: "What is a dispute for the sake of Heaven? The disputes between Hillel and Shammai" (*Ethics of the Fathers* 5:17).[5]

But, as is often the case with disputes that continue over many decades, there were less civil periods as well. Most

---

* In line with this, for example, contemporary rabbis whose standards for conversion dispense with certain ritual requirements of Jewish law should make sure to inform would-be converts that their conversions will not be acknowledged as valid by more observant Jews. That will spare these converts from later unpleasant surprises and hurts.

likely, the increase in tension between the schools intensified during the period of the first revolt against Rome (66–70 C.E.). Or it could have begun earlier, as the citizens of Judea bridled under the increasingly harsh rule of Rome.* Anxiety about how to be a Jew in dark times is something modern Jews, as well as ancient Jews, have been intimately acquainted with. A sense of the increasingly negative—and during one period, violent—relationship between the schools is suggested in a dispute between Rabbi Eliezer, the greatest scholar produced by the Shammaites, and Rabbi Joshua ben Chananiah, one of the most distinguished proponents of the Hillelite ideology.

In a ruling that sounds decidedly fair and just to modern ears, Rabbi Joshua taught that righteous non-Jews, like righteous Jews, have a share in the world to come (Tosefta *Sanhedrin* 13:2). Rabbi Eliezer ruled to the contrary, that Gentiles have no share in the world to come. Could there be a greater continuation of Hillel's decision to teach the essence of Judaism to a Gentile? Maintaining this openness to righteous Gentiles—believing that good people, whether Jewish or not, share in God's eternal rewards—during

---

* A certain potential for intolerance and even violence might have been present from the beginning. The Talmud records an episode in which Hillel went to offer a sacrifice at the Temple on a holiday in a manner that Shammai and his followers believed to be forbidden (it involved a long-standing dispute concerning laying hands on the animal that was to be offered). Hillel found himself surrounded by Shammaites and felt sufficiently threatened by them that he lied and denied his intentions (*Beitzah* 20a–b). Lying to protect oneself from attack might be permitted by Jewish law, but it certainly reveals a very unfortunate propensity for intolerance and possibly violence among at least some of Shammai's followers.

the darkness of the Roman occupation must have indeed required courage. And it must have seemed very wrong, like blasphemy, to many of those still mourning the destroyed Temple and the mass slaughter of the Jews of Jerusalem.

On one tragic day, disciples of the School of Shammai attacked, and might even have killed, members of the School of Hillel (Jerusalem Talmud, *Shabbat* 1:4). Enough Hillelites were prevented from making it to the upper chamber of the home of Chananiah ben Chizkiyah ben Garon, where the sages were meeting that day, that the School of Shammai was able to achieve what it long craved, a majority (Mishnah *Shabbat* 1:4). They took advantage of the situation to push through eighteen regulations, several of which were intended to strengthen the separation between Jews and non-Jews.

The Hillelites saw the day on which these decrees passed as "a day as grievous for Israel as the day on which the Golden Calf was made" (Jerusalem Talmud, *Shabbat* 1:4; see also *Shabbat* 17a).*

We don't know how long the Shammaites were able to maintain their dominance over the Hillelites, but we do know that the School of Hillel eventually regained its majority status—probably during the period following the failed revolt against the Romans and the destruction of the Temple.[6] It was also during this period that one of the Tal-

---

* The fact that Hillel is recorded as being present on that day, as is Shammai, is puzzling, since the events described in this passage would seem to have occurred decades after they died.

mud's most famous stories concerning a heavenly voice (*bat kol*) takes place. In the words of the Talmud:

> For three years, there was a dispute between the School of Shammai and the School of Hillel, the former asserting, "The law (*halakhah*) is according to our view," and the latter asserting, "The law is according to our view." Then, a voice issued from heaven announcing, "Both these and these are the words of the living God, but the law is in agreement with the School of Hillel."
>
> But [it was asked], since both are the words of the living God, for what reason was the School of Hillel entitled to have the law determined according to their ruling?
>
> Because they were kindly and humble, and because they studied their own rulings and those of the School of Shammai, and even mentioned the teachings of the School of Shammai before their own. (*Eruvin* 13b)

Several important, infrequently commented upon, and still applicable lessons emerge from this passage:

- There isn't necessarily *only* one way to perform a ritual act that's acceptable to God. The disputes of Hillel and Shammai were largely about issues such as purity and impurity, and matters concerning blessings, issues for which you would think that there is only one right way. Nonetheless, the heavenly voice teaches: "The teachings of both are the words of the living God."
- We should look for and seek to identify the "words of the living God" even in opinions with which we disagree.

Rabbi Irwin Kula speaks of the need to identify "partial" truths in these instances. Such an ideology must have motivated the members of the School of Hillel. Why else would they have studied Shammai's rulings, and even studied them first? Apparently, they wanted to study the reasonings of the other side. Humility also played a role in the educational agenda of each school. The Shammaites, who assumed, with a certain measure of arrogance, that they had nothing to learn from the School of Hillel, "wasted" no time studying their rulings. The more humble Hillelites did not assume that they possessed the full truth, and therefore considered opposing viewpoints. It was this that enabled them to acknowledge instances in which the Shammaite position made more sense. Humility is, therefore, not only an attractive personal attribute, it also leads to a greater grasp of the truth.

The unwillingness of the Shammaites to study and consider the Hillelites' views might explain why they later grew violent in their opposition to the School of Hillel. Associating only with like-minded people, reinforcing one another's views without ever hearing a credible exposition of opposing views, might have caused them to think that those who thought differently from them were not only wrong, but evil. A contemporary upshot of this text is that we should not read only books and publications that agree with and reinforce what we already believe. Many people do so and never learn what those who disagree with them believe. As my friend the radio talk show commentator Dennis Prager likes to say, "One of the most important days in the life of a religious person is the day he meets a person of a different religion, or of a different denomination within his own religion, who is both a good person and intelligent." After such an encounter, it becomes less easy to reflexively dismiss without consideration the arguments of the other side, or to construct superficial and unfair stereotypes of those who disagree with you. Perhaps that is why, fearing that distinctions would be blurred, the School of Shammai did not wish to study the arguments of the School of Hillel or have their students mix with people unlike themselves.

- If both sides are the words of the living God, why was one set of rulings chosen as binding? The reason would seem to be that Jewish laws aren't intended only to bring their practitioners closer to God; they are also the laws of a people, and for a people to be united, they need a unified law. (The reason why a green light signals "go" and a red light signals "stop" might or might not be arbitrary, but it is important for the safety of a people that one way is chosen and uniformly agreed upon.)

In an essay examining the teachings of Hillel and Shammai, Elie Wiesel raises the question of why it took years until a heavenly voice intervened in the debate and made a ruling. I believe that perhaps the rabbis wanted to convey that a heavenly voice should be a last resort. The goal is for the two sides in a dispute to try to convince each other through argument, and by so doing to clarify and refine their views. Only when reason has failed do we turn to a heavenly voice.*

---

* Rabbi David Woznica suggests that "perhaps the heavenly voice intervenes as a last resort so that the dispute would not escalate into something more, and worse, than verbal."

And even then, we see that the heavenly voice does not speak in an authoritarian tone. Even as the heavenly voice comes to tell us that we should follow the rulings of Hillel, it also affirms that there is more than one path to truth.

In point of fact, the whole issue of the intervening heavenly voice is a problematic one. Indeed, as well known as this story of the heavenly voice favoring Hillel over Shammai is, there is a second, even more famous story in the Talmud about another heavenly voice. And this other story reaches precisely the opposite conclusion. This story is told about the previously mentioned Shammaite scholar, Rabbi Eliezer ben Hyrcanus, whose scholarship was recognized by Hillelite rabbis as well. The Talmud relates:

> On that day, Rabbi Eliezer put forward all the arguments in the world, but the Sages did not accept them. Finally, he said to them, "If the law is according to me, let that carob tree prove it." He pointed to a nearby carob tree, which then moved from its place a hundred cubits, and some say, four hundred cubits.
>
> They said to him, "One cannot bring a proof from the moving of a carob tree." Said Rabbi Eliezer, "If the law is according to me, may that stream of water prove it." The stream of water then turned and flowed in the opposite direction. They said to him, "One cannot bring a proof from the behavior of a stream of water."

Said Rabbi Eliezer, "If the law is according to me, may the walls of the House of Study prove it." The walls of the House of Study began to bend inwards. Rabbi Joshua then rose up and rebuked the walls of the House of Study: "If the students of the wise argue with one another in matters of Jewish law," he said, "what right have you to interfere?"

In honor of Rabbi Joshua, the walls ceased to bend inwards; but in honor of Rabbi Eliezer, they did not straighten up, and they remain bent to this day.

Then said Rabbi Eliezer to the Sages, "If the law is according to me, may a proof come from Heaven." Then, a heavenly voice came forth and said, "What have you to do with Rabbi Eliezer? The law is according to him in every place."

Then Rabbi Joshua rose up on his feet and said, "It is not in the heavens" [a quote from Deut. 30:12].

What did he mean by quoting this? Said Rabbi Jeremiah, "He meant that since the Torah has already been given on Mount Sinai, we do not pay attention to a heavenly voice, for God Himself has written in the Torah, 'Decide according to the majority'" (Exod. 23:2).

Rabbi Nathan met the prophet Elijah. He asked him, "What was the Holy One, blessed be He, doing in that hour?" [that is, while this was happening].

Said Elijah, "He was laughing and saying, 'My children have defeated me, my children have defeated me.'" (*Bava Metzia* 59b)

That divine voice communicated to Rabbi Nathan, through the prophet Elijah, the same message of anti-fundamentalism as was related in the earlier story, regarding Rabbi Eliezer, in which the divine voice is heard.

Hillel, who so esteemed logic, probably would have wanted to have his positions chosen on the basis of logic and majority rule, rather than on the basis of a divine voice.* But there are others, as we know, who prefer divine voices and miracles. Perhaps this passage is intended to teach us that God is on the side of those who are humble, who are willing to learn from their opponents, and who accord respect to those who disagree with them.

Certainly these are the traits we associate with Hillel. And yet, while Hillel is continually supported by the Talmud, racking up victory after victory in legalistic skirmishes, and is honored in our time as a revered sage, he remains the historical loser in a larger conflict with the spirit of Shammai in ways we have only begun to reckon with (see, for example, pp. 171–172).

The danger, as identified in the Talmud, comes when there is an increase in the number of disciples of Shammai and Hillel "who had insufficiently studied with them." It is because of the ignorance of those invoking the names of Hillel and Shammai without truly knowing them that "disputes proliferated in Israel and the Torah became as two Torahs."

---

* The late professor Ephraim Urbach argued that the School of Hillel's rulings were indeed chosen on the basis of majority rule (not a divine voice) because, as the story with Rabbi Eliezer demonstrates, a *bat kol* is ignored "when it does not reflect the majority opinion" (*The Halakhah*, p. 268).

It is my hope in this book that by presenting Hillel and Shammai together, the reader will have a chance to study them and, in a sense, study with them. Only then can the healing of the houses, and what those houses represent, truly take place.

PART III

Hillel and Jesus

12

The Jewish Sage
and the Christian Messiah

Hillel and Shammai are the Talmud's most famous pair but it is impossible to talk about Hillel without considering another figure who quickly came to overshadow him in world history, despite having been born after Hillel and having most probably been influenced by him. That figure is Jesus. The two men, both of whom lived in the first century—though Hillel is two generations older*—are frequently compared, and it is worth considering them briefly side by side. Just as Shammai is at times cast unfairly in the role of inflexible literalist when compared with Hillel, so has Hillel often been cast, very unfairly, in a similar role when compared by some Christian scholars with Jesus.

In a famous New Testament passage, Jesus is pressed to declare what he regards as the Torah's greatest commandment. Jesus cites two verses: "You shall love the Lord your

---

* Hillel lived most of his life in the first century B.C.E. and is presumed to have died in about 10 C.E.

God"* and "Love your neighbor as yourself" (Matt. 22:37–40). Elsewhere, he says, "So always treat others as you would like them to treat you; that is the meaning of the Law and the Prophets" (Matt. 7:12). Jesus' citing of the law of love of neighbor and the Golden Rule have been frequently contrasted with Hillel's seemingly negative summation of Judaism's essence, "What is hateful unto you, do not do to your neighbor." More than a few Christian scholars have argued that Jesus' positive formulation represents a higher ethic than Hillel's.†

In the case of Jesus' and Hillel's statements of religion's essence, comparisons are particularly unwise because the teaching "Love your neighbor as yourself" did not originate with Jesus, as many Christians believe. Nor did Jesus think he was being original in making this statement. Rather, he was simply quoting a verse from the Hebrew Bible (Lev. 19:18), in which the commandment to love one's neighbor is set down for the first time.

But comparisons between Hillel's and Jesus' teachings on a number of issues can be fruitful. For one thing, it is valuable for Christian scholars to bring Hillel into a consideration of Jesus because of his likely influence on the figure at the center of their religion. Jesus was raised as a Jew and grew up among Jews, and Hillel was the most significant religious figure in the Jewish community during Jesus'

---

* The words "You shall love the Lord your God" (Deut. 6:5) form part of the Shema prayer, which Jews are instructed to recite twice daily.

† As regards why Hillel might have offered a negative formulation of this verse, see pp. 20–23.

youth. That Jesus would have been familiar with Hillel—and with some of his more famous teachings—can be assumed.

Comparisons between teachings of Hillel and Jesus can be beneficial for Jews as well, because it is quite possible that, in later centuries, anxiety about the revolution wrought in Jesus' name spawned anxiety about those aspects of Hillel's teachings—the extraordinary openness to converts and the emphasis on loving and just behavior as God's central demand—that, though older than Christianity, suddenly sounded strangely un-Jewish.

It was perhaps in response to Jesus' emphasis on faith and love, and Paul's decision several decades later to drop the requirement to observe Torah laws,[1] that many Jews came to focus Jewish religiosity on laws, specifically the ritual laws that most differentiated Jews from Gentiles. For example, if two Jews are speaking about a third, and the question "Is so-and-so religious?" is raised, the answer is based exclusively on the person's level of ritual observance. Such a standard is, of course, precisely the opposite of what Hillel taught about Judaism's essence.

All of this is not meant to suggest that Hillel was not concerned with ritual observance. He was. Very. Indeed, most of the disputes between Shammai and him and among their disciples were on matters of ritual law. He simply deemed Judaism's ethical demands to be foremost in significance, and it is one of the paradoxes of history that the very power of Hillel's moral teaching, having likely affected Jesus, his disciples, and the religion founded in his name, might have been responsible for provoking an anxiety about those very teachings in Jews who felt threatened by the rise and growing popularity of Christianity—a feeling that intensified after Christianity had done away with the legal structure of the Torah and started to hold Jews accountable for their savior's death.

But it is infrequently noted that Jesus, unlike Paul, believed in the binding nature of Torah law as well: "Do not imagine that I have come to abolish the Law [the Torah] or the Prophets," he told his disciples. "I tell you solemnly, until heaven and earth disappear, not one dot, not one little stroke, shall disappear from the Law until its purpose is achieved." The law's "purpose" of course is the universal recognition of God, a goal that neither Christianity nor Judaism believes was realized in Jesus' time or since. Jesus concluded his message with a severe warning: "Therefore, the man who infringes even the least of these commandments and teaches others to do the same will be considered the least in the kingdom of heaven" (Matt. 5:17–19).*

In addition to their ethical emphases, there are a few other striking similarities between Hillel and Jesus. Both lived in economically trying circumstances and worked as manual laborers: Hillel, according to one account, as a woodchopper and Jesus as a carpenter.

More striking, however, are their differences. The central feature in Hillel's aphorisms is his emphasis on Torah study, the subject of so many of his teachings ("Do not say, 'When

---

* Jesus does reveal on a number of occasions a more lax attitude on the observance of several rituals related to Sabbath observance.

I have [free] time, I will study,' lest you never have [free] time." "An ignorant person cannot be a saint.") and the nonelitist attitude of his disciples ("One should teach any person, for there were many sinners in Israel, yet when they drew close to the study of Torah, there issued from them men who were righteous, saintly, and worthy.")*

For Hillel, study was the essential prerequisite for knowing and fulfilling one's obligations, because virtue is not achieved through good intentions alone. Good intentions need be coupled with ongoing and vigorous intellectual effort. The late Jewish scholar Hyam Maccoby commented that "learning was regarded as the duty of every Jew and as the basis of all useful and virtuous living."[2]

But central as Torah study is to Hillel, what one does not find in his aphorisms are teachings about God and about prayer. There are no statements such as "Do not say, 'When I have free time, I will pray,' lest you never have free time," or even "One who does not believe in God cannot be a fully righteous person." A passionate believer in Torah—and in the God to whom he attributed its authorship—Hillel almost never speaks, at least in the passages the rabbis transmit in his name, about God.† In one of his classical formulations, he declares, "Be of the disciples of Aaron . . . one who loves people and brings them close to Torah" (*Ethics of the Fathers* 1:12). "Close to Torah" is what he says, not "close to God." Similarly, in the instances of the non-Jews who

---

* For further discussion of these passages, see chapters 13 and 16.
† I am indebted for this insight to Alon Goshen-Gottstein, "Hillel and Jesus: Are Comparisons Possible?" in James Charlesworth and Loren Johns, eds., *Hillel and Jesus: Comparisons of Two Major Religious Leaders*, pp. 50–53.

come to him seeking to convert (see chapters 3 and 4), Hillel emphasizes to each the importance of Torah and of study, and does not speak of God (presumably he assumed, based on their interest in converting, that they already held such a belief).

On the subject of prayer, Hillel is silent as well. His and Shammai's disciples debated whether or not a person has to stand in the morning when reciting the Shema, but one looks in vain for teachings of Hillel about the experience of prayer itself. He was a man of deep, but rarely discussed, faith. The Talmud records that once, on his way home, Hillel heard loud shouts coming from the direction of his neighborhood, but he did not offer a prayer. Instead, he declared, "I am confident that this screaming is not taking place within my house" (*Berakhot* 60a). Perhaps Hillel believed that prayer at such a time would be what is called in Hebrew a *berakhah le-vatalah*, a pointless prayer. Once you've heard the cries, it is too late to pray that the shouts are not coming from your home. Either they are, or they aren't (see Mishnah *Berakhot* 9:3). Nonetheless, and despite Hillel's attitude of great calm, I find that such prayers are still commonly offered, and I would probably find myself among those who pray at such a moment.

In contrast to Hillel, one looks in vain in the New Testament for statements from Jesus advocating rigorous Bible study.* It is not intellectual sophistication that Jesus seems

---

* I am not a New Testament scholar, so I hope my generalization is not overly broad. The advocacy of study, though, is clearly not a theme associated with Jesus.

to value most, but simple faith: "I tell you solemnly, unless you change and become like little children, you will never enter the kingdom of heaven" (Matt. 18:3). Jesus speaks about the experience of prayer often. In particular, he extols private prayers: "But when you pray, go to your private room and, when you have shut your door, pray to your Father" (Matt. 6:6). When the prayer is not offered by an individual, Jesus favors praying in small groups (Matt. 18:20). The most famous prayer associated with Jesus, which begins with "Our Father who are in heaven," is set down in Matthew (6:10–13) and known to this day by Christians as the Lord's Prayer. Jesus also believed prayer to be singularly effective in procuring one's needs: "Ask, and it will be given to you . . . your Father in heaven [will] give good things to those who ask him!" (Matt. 7:7, 11). This is a belief that is certainly common among religious Jews as well, but one that is not found in the corpus of Hillel's teachings. And, of course, Jesus speaks repeatedly about God and the soon-to-come kingdom of heaven.

The New Testament also cites several teachings distinctive to Jesus, and for which one finds no parallels in Hillel's words, or in Jewish theology in general. Three such statements are particularly significant for they have characterized Christian theology ever since:

• Jesus forgives all sins: "The Son of man has the authority to forgive sins" (Matt. 9:6). Traditional Jewish theology teaches that not even God Himself forgives all sins, only those sins committed against Him alone. As the Mishnah teaches: "The Day of Atonement atones for sins against God, not for sins committed against man, unless the injured party has been appeased" (Mishnah *Yoma* 8:9).

- Jesus was an ardent pacifist and commanded his followers to love the oppressor: "Offer the wicked man no resistance. On the contrary, if anyone hits you on the right cheek, offer him the other as well" (Matt. 5:39), and "Love your enemies and pray for your persecutors" (Matt. 5:44). In contrast, Judaism demands that the wicked be offered powerful resistance. Only three events are recorded about Moses before God chooses him to be Israel's leader, the first of which is his killing an Egyptian overseer who is beating an Israelite slave (Exod. 2:12). Moses obviously deemed it important to resist the wicked. In addition, Judaism does not demand that one love one's enemies, though it is untrue to claim, as Matthew does, that Jewish law commands one to hate one's enemies (see Matt. 5:43). What the Torah and later biblical writings insist on is justice, not love, toward one's enemies. For example, if you see your enemy's donkey lying down under its burden, you are commanded to help him raise the animal (Exod. 23:5). If your enemy is hungry, you are instructed to feed him (Prov. 25:21).

- Jesus claimed that people can come to God only through him: "No one knows the Father except the Son, and anyone to whom the Son chooses to reveal Him" (Matt. 11:27). In contrast, the Hebrew Bible teaches—in a psalm recited by observant Jews at two of the three daily prayers services—that "God is near to all who call unto Him"

(Pss. 145:18). The Jewish teaching is that one can approach God directly without an intermediary, whereas the belief of many Christians to this day is that one can come to God only through Jesus.*

In addition to the different aspects of religiosity new Christians chose to emphasize, Jesus' personality and teaching persona are also quite dissimilar from Hillel's. Most significantly, Jesus is portrayed as a healer and a miracle worker. The healings attributed to him in the New Testament are manifold: he is depicted as curing a leper (Matt. 8:2–3), a paralyzed man (Matt. 9:1–8), two blind men (Matt. 9:27–31), and a deaf man (Mark 7:31–37), among others. He is credited with performing additional miracles as well, the most famous of which is walking on water (Mark 6:45–52). No healings or miracles are attributed to Hillel.

It is, however, in the context of Jesus' healing acts that an unexpected aspect of his personality emerges. According to a widely ignored passage in the Gospels of Matthew and Mark, it would appear that Jesus—unlike Hillel—might well have identified with the most nationalistic and anti-Gentile camps within the Jewish community. Matthew relates an incident in which Jesus is walking with his disciples in the northern areas of Tyre and Sidon.

Then out came a Canaanite woman from that district and started shouting, "Sir, Son of David, take pity on

* See Dennis Prager and Joseph Telushkin, *The Nine Questions People Ask About Judaism*, pp. 85–87.

me. My daughter is tormented by a devil." But he answered her not a word. And his disciples went and pleaded with him: "Give her what she wants," they said, "because she is shouting after us." He said in reply, "I was sent only to the lost sheep of Israel." But the woman had come up and was kneeling at his feet. "Lord," she said, "help me." He replied, "It is not fair to take the children's food and throw it to the house-dogs." She retorted, "Ah, yes, sir, but even house-dogs can eat the scraps that fall from their master's table." Then Jesus answered her, "Woman, you have great faith. Let your wish be granted." (Matt. 15:21–28; see also Mark 7:24–30)

In this instance, Jesus is moved by the woman's great faith in his abilities, but his general estimation of and concern for non-Jews seems to be very low. (Later on, and in contrast, Jesus is depicted as instructing his disciples to spread his message among the Gentiles.)

There are other differences as well between the two men. Hillel becomes the leader of his generation and the object of great acclaim. Jesus remains the leader of a small band of followers and seems to have been widely rejected by the broader society during his lifetime (though obviously, his teachings subsequently went on to become extraordinarily influential and have affected billions of people). Perhaps the most fundamental personality difference between the two men is that Hillel is a moderate by nature, for all the radical implications of several of his teachings; Jesus is a radical by disposition, one who often phrases his demands in the stark-est of terms: "If anyone comes to me without hating his own father, mother, wife, children, brothers, sisters, yes, and his own life too, he cannot be my disciple" (Luke 14:26). Put these words in Hillel's mouth, and they sound inconceivable. Yet Jesus, it would seem, meant these teachings to be taken quite seriously, though presumably not literally. When a young man instructed by Jesus to follow him responds, "Let me go first and bury my father," Jesus answers, "Let the dead bury the dead. Your duty is to go and spread the news of the kingdom of God" (Luke 9:59–60). Obviously no act will so alienate a child from his family as not attending his father's funeral. Once again, it is impossible to imagine Hillel demanding this of a follower.

Jesus' lack of moderation carried over to the realm of money. The Gospel of Mark tells of a young man who asks Jesus what he need do to inherit eternal life. Jesus enumer-ates several of the Ten Commandments, then adds, "There is one thing you lack. Go and sell everything you own and give the money to the poor" (Mark 10:21–22). In contrast, Hillel's demands concerning the afterlife are more restrained: "One who acquires for himself Torah acquires for himself the life of the world to come" (*Ethics of the Fathers* 2:8).* As regards divesting oneself of all of one's assets for

---

* On one issue in particular, divorce—which biblical law vested in the hands of the husband—Jesus' teaching seems aligned to the position of the Sham-maites, who ruled that the only ground for divorce was sexual betrayal (see p. 98 and Matt. 5:31–32). Hillel permitted a man to divorce his wife for any reason whatsoever (in effect, favoring the rights of the husband over that of the wife; see p. 113).

charity, the Talmud ruled that one should not give away to charity more than 20 percent of one's income (*Ketubot* 50a); the rabbis did not want a charitable person to end up being in need of charity himself.

Comparisons between Hillel and Jesus are inevitable, but will always be unsatisfactory because they inhabited two different religious spheres. Jesus (as is true of Hillel) is known from documents written after his death and after the destruction of the Temple, when the Temple sacrifices and worship of Hillel's time had ceased and religious practices had undergone a radical shift. Jesus' story was largely told by people who saw him as the originator of a new faith, not as one who saw himself as part of an old one. Stripped of his Jewish context—which many New Testament scholars have in recent years worked hard to restore—Jesus appears as the radical founder of a new religion. Hillel himself might have seemed to represent a fork in the Jewish road were he not presented inside a Talmudic culture that allowed radical disagreements and alternatives their place within Judaism.

It may be easy for Jews to say that what is true in Jesus' teachings is not new (e.g., the emphasis on loving one's neighbor and loving God), and what is new in his teachings is not true (e.g., the injunction to "offer the wicked man no resistance," and the claim that he has the authority to forgive sins). But just as many New Testament scholars have been restoring the Jewish context of Jesus, so it seems appropriate for Jews to acknowledge not only that aspects of Jewish culture made their way powerfully into the teachings of Jesus, but that the openness Christianity displays to Gentiles was already comfortably embraced by Hillel long before Jesus had preached his first sermon.*

---

* Is there a Jewish consensus on how Jews are to regard Jesus? Perhaps not, but no Jewish scholars with whom I am familiar believe that Jesus intended to start a new religion.

PART IV

Lessons from the First Century
for the Twenty-first Century—
and Beyond

13

"Teach Everyone": Outreach in the First Century

The School of Shammai's approach is insular. Make sure to keep those already in the fold inside, and be very cautious before letting in others who might contaminate them. The Hillelites' approach is inclusive. The Torah should not be seen as blessing the lives only of those who already possess it, but as offering life lessons and transformational teachings to everyone to whom it is conveyed. Hillel was essentially the earliest, or most prominent, advocate of outreach. No debate so highlights the difference between these two approaches—a difference that has enduring ramifications for the Jewish people today—as the argument between the schools as to which students should be admitted:

"The School of Shammai says: One should teach only one who is wise and humble, of good family and rich; but the School of Hillel says: One should teach any person, for there were many sinners in Israel who were brought near [to God] by studying Torah, and from whom descended righteous, pious, and honorable people" (*The Fathers According to Rabbi Nathan* 2:9).

Though phrased in terms of positive attributes, the Shammaites' underlying concern is to find reasons to exclude people. Reflect for a moment on the first demands they impose on applicants—wisdom and humility—and it seems as if they wish only to teach those who have already incorporated two of the most important lessons to be learned from the Torah. Additional years of study might deepen a person's wisdom and humility, but the basic prerequisite traits must already be there for the Shammaites to be willing to admit him. Regarding the third requirement, good family background, this is definitely an asset, but what are those who don't come from a distinguished background to do? Are they to be excluded from a life of study because of a factor over which they have no control? And then there is that strange and disturbing demand of wealth. We've already seen that they didn't want their students to learn the teachings of Hillel and his followers; now it seems that they didn't want them to relate in any but the most superficial way with anyone outside of their circles.

In addition, the requirement of wealth* seems almost to have been directed at Hillel who, as noted, enters Jewish consciousness as a poor man who comes to study Torah, and who is initially denied the opportunity to do so by a school

---

* Professor Shmuel Safrai argues that the word used for "rich" (*ashir*) is a copyist's error, and the Shammaites actually spoke of admitting only those who were *kasher*, "virtuous" (Shmuel Safrai, *The Literature of the Sages*, p. 188). If Safrai is correct, and the majority of scholars who have written on the subject do not assume this to be the case, the Shammaites' attitude would still be elitist, but would not discriminate on the basis of wealth.

gatekeeper who bars him from entrance until he makes a daily payment; in Hillel's case, the payment comprises half of his earnings. The fact that Hillel was a day laborer who rose to become the most prominent rabbi of his age must have been known to Shammai's disciples. That they were willing to exclude poor Jews from advanced educational opportunities might have reflected a lingering bitterness at Hillel and at the great acceptance accorded him by the Jewish masses.

If the House of Shammai's statement was indeed a sly critique of Hillel, it is likely not the only time we find this sort of tactic used in Talmudic literature. Consider the only teaching in the Mishnah attributed to Rabbi Elisha ben Abuyah (first–second century C.E.). An infamous figure among the rabbis, Elisha came from a distinguished and wealthy family, grew up to become a scholar of renown, and then, during a midlife crisis of faith, became a religious heretic and an admirer and supporter of the Romans, the rulers and oppressors of Judea.[1] Nonetheless, when *Ethics of the Fathers* was compiled, the rabbis saw fit to include in it a teaching of Elisha's on the seemingly innocuous topic of the importance of educating children when they are young: "He who learns as a child, to what may he be compared? To ink written down on new paper. And he who learns while old, to what may he be compared? To ink written on used paper" (*Ethics of the Fathers* 4:20).

The greatest sage of Elisha's age was Rabbi Akiva, who started out as a poor shepherd and did not have the opportunity to study Torah until he was forty. Was Elisha's mockery of those who start their learning at an advanced age directed at Rabbi Akiva? This is certainly a reasonable hypothesis (much as if a presidential candidate in the United States in 1860 who ridiculed those born in log cabins would have been suspected of mocking Abraham Lincoln).

There might well be a tinge of rabbinic irony, directed against Elisha himself, in including his provocative comment. Elisha, who learned Torah from a young age, ended up a heretic and an enemy of the Jews, whereas Akiva, whose study commenced at a relatively old age, ranks alongside Hillel in his enduring impact on Jewish law and life.

What, therefore, was the rationale of Shammai's disciples in excluding the poor from the study of Torah? We know that in the Greek and Roman world, higher study was confined to the upper classes and perhaps, knowingly or unknowingly, the Shammaites were influenced by this elitist attitude. Another possible rationale: the study of Torah requires an enormous amount of time, many hours a day for many years; therefore, it made sense to them to open it up only to those who had the financial security to devote large amounts of time to this study.

A counterview, offered anonymously, is recorded in the Talmudic tractate *Nedarim* (81a): "Be careful [not to neglect] the children of the poor, for from them Torah will go forth." The contemporary Israeli Talmudic scholar and commentator Rabbi Adin Steinsaltz argues that the author of this statement is none other than Hillel, and that it was Hillel who abolished tuition at the Jewish academies.[2] He apparently didn't want people excluded from study as he had been, an exclusion that had almost cost him his life (see p. 4).[3]

What shines through in the teachings of Hillel and his disciples' is a fundamental optimism about human nature and the capacity of Torah to affect people positively. It is not just that they don't want the poor discriminated against; they don't want anybody discriminated against, sinners, too. Let everyone be offered the teachings of the Torah, so that their lives can be shaped by them. From Hillel's perspective, Shammai's attitude would be like a hospital administrator admitting only healthy people for examination. Such a policy might make life easier on the hospital staff, but that is not the hospital's purpose. If Torah has something to teach the world, its message cannot be restricted to those elite few who have already incorporated its teachings.

Once again, Hillel's teaching has an important message to convey to modern Jews: Jewish schools must have generous admissions policies that enable students to attend who are from noncommitted backgrounds (in terms of Jewish observance) or who cannot pay high tuitions.

Has the House of Hillel's position triumphed on this issue, or has that of the House of Shammai? In theory, certainly Hillel's. The spirit of the Talmud and of later Jewish writings on education is that Torah must be accessible to everyone. In modern Israel, where the public school system includes religious schools, Hillel's approach has certainly been incorporated. But in the Diaspora, where children's Jewish education must be financed by the parents—and limited funds are available for scholarships—it is not clear that this has been the case. Unfortunately, the final part of Shammai's statement, on educating affluent people from good family backgrounds, has been more the norm. Sadly, poor people from unimpressive family backgrounds still find it difficult to get a comprehensive Jewish education.

The consequences of this policy have been unfortunate. How many other Hillels have there been, their noses pressed against the window, who have never been admitted to Jewish study? We will never know. And yet, had the Shammaites' policy prevailed in ancient Israel, we would not have had Hillel, and a century later we would not have had Rabbi Akiva. Had elitist policies prevailed in nineteenth-century America, we would not have had Abraham Lincoln as president. That Judaism would have been so different a religion without Hillel, and the United States so different a country without Lincoln, serves to remind us how important Hillel's instruction to "teach everyone" was, not only in his day but in ours as well.

14

"The Highly Impatient Person Cannot Teach": For Today's Teachers and Parents

Probably few people in the ancient world (and even in the modern world until recently) focused, as did Hillel, on how disqualifying a trait a teacher's angry disposition should be. In the Talmud, strictness in educational matters—including physical discipline—was generally esteemed and, on occasion, behavior that should have been regarded as criminal was condoned. The most painful passage I am familiar with in the Mishnah is the ruling in *Makkot* (2:2) exonerating from punishment a teacher who unintentionally kills a student while disciplining him.

How ironic that in the face of so potentially harsh an educational system, Hillel's sensitive teaching is frequently cited. There are few Jews conversant with Jewish texts who are unfamiliar with Hillel's three-word dictum, *lo ha-kapdan lamed*, "The highly impatient (alternatively 'overly strict') person cannot teach." (*Ethics of the Fathers* 2:5)

But while Hillel's statement gained currency in the popular mind, it made few inroads in Jewish law. The ruling about the teacher who kills a student was codified as official Jewish law a full two hundred years after Hillel.[1] A millennium later, Maimonides incorporated this ruling into his code of Jewish law, along with the rationale that punishment is not inflicted on the homicidal teacher since the killing was done unintentionally and "while performing a mitzvah" (*Mishneh Torah*, "Laws of Murder and Guarding of Life" 5:6).* Some mitzvah!

What kinds of punishments did a ruling of this sort justify? Harsh ones, we can imagine, since nobody ever died from a lightly administered slap (which I am not justifying, either). But in addition to Hillel's dictum about impatient teachers, the Talmud also contained some relatively enlightened rulings regarding corporal punishment, for example, "If you [feel you] must strike a child, hit him only with a shoelace" (*Bava Batra* 21a).

Hillel's teaching is more than a humanitarian sentiment; it also contains profound pedagogical wisdom, the sort ignored by those who favor harsh discipline. If the goal of teaching is to impart knowledge and to develop a mind, when is that more likely to occur, in an atmosphere of fear and punishment, or one of calmness and kindness? Fear limits what students can learn, most obviously because a teacher's bad temper will cause students to be reluctant to ask questions, out of concern that doing so will evoke the teacher's wrath. Consequently, students of bad-tempered

---

*The mitzvah referred to is the teaching of Torah.

teachers are less likely to come out of the classroom understanding the material they have been taught. As yet another
Talmudic text—in line with the thinking of Hillel—taught:
"Rava said: 'If you see a student whose studies are as hard
for him as iron, attribute it to his teacher's failure to show
him a cheerful countenance' " (*Ta'anit* 8a).

I do not cite this earlier Mishnaic ruling to suggest that
the Jewish classroom was the scene of more brutal punishments than those that prevailed in non-Jewish societies. We
have enough accounts from non-Jewish writers of the cruel-
ties perpetrated by teachers in Christian, Muslim, and secular schools to not cast Jewish schools into a worse light. Here
is an early reminiscence of the fourth-century Saint Augustine: "I was sent to school in order to read. I was too young
to understand what the purpose of the whole thing was, and
nevertheless if I was idle in my studies, I was flogged."

The fact that a man like Hillel so strongly advocated a
kinder type of pedagogy—and that his words were so commonly disregarded—should not be overlooked or mini-
mized. Nineteen centuries after Hillel, Chayyim Nachman
Bialik, the great Hebrew poet, described in frightening
detail how the harsh discipline in Jewish schools appeared to
him as a young student:

[The teachers] knew only to hurt, each in his own way.
The rebbe used to hit with a whip, with his fist, with
his elbow, with his wife's rolling pin, or with anything
else that would cause pain. But his assistant, whenever
my answer to his questions was wrong, would advance

toward me, with the fingers of his palm extended, and bend before my face and seize me by my throat. He would look to me then like a leopard or tiger or some other such wild beast and I would be in mortal dread. I was afraid he would gouge out my eyes with his dirty fingernails and the fear would paralyze my mind so that I forgot everything I had learned the previous day.

It is even more horrifying to realize that the recipients of the sorts of punishments described in these passages must often have been children with learning disabilities or attention disorders like ADD or ADHD. Imagine a system in which deaf people were punished for not hearing and the blind for not seeing, then imagine a system in which a child with dyslexia was slapped or beaten for not reading properly.

It is rarely noted that harsh school discipline played a role in the mass defection from religious commitment of the late-nineteenth- and early-twentieth-century eastern European Jews. When I was growing up in the 1950s, I encountered many elderly Jewish immigrants; few had nostalgic memories of the *cheders* (Jewish elementary schools) they had attended in eastern Europe. Instead, they frequently commented upon the cruel discipline they had suffered.

I also wonder whether Hillel, in dismissing a *kapdan* as a teacher, was also getting in a sly "dig" at his rival Shammai. In rabbinic literature, the word *kapdan* is associated on more than one occasion with Shammai. A Talmudic text that lauds Hillel's patience begins by saying, "A man should always be humble [and gentle] like Hillel, and not a *kapdan* like Shammai." The rather lengthy passage about the three converts ends with the men mutually concluding that "*kap-danuto* [the angry impatience] of Shammai sought to drive us out of the world" (*Shabbat* 31a).

Yet again, we see that although Hillel was appreciated in the abstract, and his teaching repeatedly cited and widely known by heart, he was too often ignored. Today, happily, the beating of students in Jewish schools is a thing of the past. But Hillel's dictum still applies, for there are many ways other than physical punishment in which ill-tempered people cause great damage to their students. Those who are sarcastic, those who humiliate with cruel, ridiculing words,[2] those who create an environment in which students fear to ask questions or to admit that they don't understand what has been taught, are not fit to teach Judaism in an age of inclusion. In truth they never were, and it is to Hillel's credit that he recognized this *two millennia ago*—at a time when almost no one else did.

15

"One Who Is Bashful
Will Never Learn":
Why It Is Essential to Question

Hillel clearly was not an aggressive person. His patience was legendary. In only two of the many encounters recorded between Hillel and others do we find him offering a sharp retort.[1]

The Talmudic tradition hails bashfulness as a lauded trait, and one that characterizes the ideal Jew: "This people [Israel] are distinguished by three characteristics: They are merciful, bashful, and perform acts of kindness" (*Yevamot* 79a). However, there is one area in which bashfulness is not a virtue: study.* There, it is a great disadvantage because it intimidates the learner and keeps him or her from asking questions, clarifying issues, and challenging the teacher (and, by implication, any authority figures). This teaching by Hillel is widely known and has exerted, I believe, an enormous impact on Jewish learning. For example, a Talmudic passage describes the relationship between the third-

* Hillel, *Ethics of the Fathers* 2:5.

century rabbi Yochanan and his leading student, Resh Lakish. The two men studied together for many years, but then had a terrible falling-out. During this period, Resh Lakish, likely overwhelmed with depression at the loss of the friendship, became sick and died. Then Rabbi Yochanan fell into a depression, and the rabbis sent him a brilliant young student, Rabbi Elazar ben Pedat, to divert him from his grief. The plan didn't work, specifically because Rabbi Elazar, likely in awe of Rabbi Yochanan, didn't challenge his teachings. Whenever Rabbi Yochanan uttered an opinion, Rabbi Elazar, whose knowledge was encyclopedic, would say, "I know another source that supports what you are saying."

Rabbi Yochanan finally said to him, "Whenever I stated an opinion, Resh Lakish would raise twenty-four objections to what I was saying. . . . He forced me to justify every ruling I gave, so that in the end the subject was fully clarified. But all you do is tell me that you know another source that supports what I am saying. Don't I know myself that what I have said is right?" (*Bava Metzia* 84a).

It is the questioning student who will grow, and who will also prompt growth in his teacher. The Talmud relates that Resh Lakish had grown up among the lowest sort of people. One text even suggests that he was raised in a gang that used to purchase men to participate in gladiator fights, and Rabbi Adin Steinsaltz argues that Resh Lakish, legendary for his great physical strength, was himself a gladiator.[2] In any case, after years of studying with, questioning, and challenging Rabbi Yochanan, Resh Lakish grew into one of the great sages of his time.

The approach put forth here by Hillel, disparaging bashfulness as a bad trait in students (and, by implication, commending students for challenging teachers), has continued to be advocated by Judaism's greatest teachers. Rabbi Norman Lamm, the longtime president of Yeshiva University, recalls that when he was a new student in Rabbi Joseph Soloveitchik's Talmud *shiur*, the most advanced Talmud class at Yeshiva University, Rabbi Soloveitchik asked him to summarize the approach of Tosafot (a medieval commentary) to a passage the class had been studying. The young Lamm, thinking to please his teacher, repeated the explanation of the passage Rabbi Soloveitchik had offered the previous day. But instead of being pleased, the rabbi said to Lamm, "I know what I am saying. I do not need you to tell me. What do *you* think? . . . The problem is that you check your evil inclination (*yetzer hara*) outside the classroom door and come in with your good inclination. Next time, bring your evil inclination with you, and leave your good inclination outside."[3]

Rabbi Soloveitchik wanted students not to be intimidated by his reputation as a great Talmudist, but to challenge him. Without such challenges, the student becomes at best a receptacle for the teacher's wisdom. And such an attitude denies the teacher an opportunity to deepen his own understanding. A Talmudic aphorism quotes the sage Rabbi Chanina, "I have learned much from my teachers, and from my colleagues more than from my teachers, and from my students more than from them all" (*Ta'anit* 7a). When students question and pose challenges to their teachers—as Resh Lakish did to Rabbi Yochanan—they grow and the teacher grows.

In line with Hillel's teaching, the *Shulchan Arukh*, the

landmark sixteenth-century code of Jewish law, ruled: "A student should not be embarrassed if a fellow student has understood something after the first and second time, but he himself has not grasped it even after several attempts. If he is embarrassed because of this, it will turn out that he will come and go from the house of study without learning anything at all." Even worse, he might form an erroneous impression and pass his misinformation on to others.

Hillel's insistence on pushing students to overcome their timidity in the classroom setting has characterized Jewish life, both religious and secular, ever since. Arthur Sackler, a friend of the late Isador Rabi's, the noted Nobel laureate in physics, once asked him, "Why did you become a scientist, rather than a doctor or lawyer or businessman, like the other immigrant kids in your neighborhood?"

Rabi answered: "My mother made me a scientist without ever intending it. Every other Jewish mother in Brooklyn would ask her child after school, 'So, did you learn anything today?' But not my mother. She always asked me a different question. 'Izzy,' she would say, 'did you ask a good question today?' That difference, asking good questions, made me become a scientist.' "

The first words most Jewish children speak in a public setting are the *Mah Nishtanah*, the "Four Questions" recited at the Passover seder. Even a timid child is prodded to stand up and recite the questions.

All this, I believe, goes back in large part to Hillel's brief aphorism and his understanding that the price paid for bashfulness and timidity—knowledge itself—is too high.

This belief is also what may have allowed Hillel to

embrace not only the impatient convert but also the man's challenge to impart the essence of Judaism in a simple encapsulated lesson. The famous seeker did not leave his "evil inclination" at the door, issuing instead the ultimate challenge to a religion of vast learning, endless disputation, and elaborate ritual. And yet out of that challenge grew a formulation of Judaism we are still trying to fulfill. Who is to say that Hillel did not learn as much from that "student" as he learned from his teachers and colleagues?

16

"Do Not Say, 'When I Have [Free] Time, I Will Study,' Lest You Never Have [Free] Time": The Eternal Challenge

Hillel was very concerned that a large percentage of the population be engaged in study, for he believed in the power of Torah to transform each student's life. But he also understood that most of his fellow Jews were poor and needed to devote the large part of their waking hours to earning a living. Tell such people that they must make time for ongoing Torah study and, Hillel knew, the response would be something like, "Perhaps in a few years, when I no longer have to work so hard, I will have time to study."

As we saw in his interactions with the three proselytes, Hillel was a master pedagogue, one who could anticipate people's objections and arguments. In this case, he understood that the types of excuses offered for not studying would always apply. How many of us have found that our lives have become less busy over time, and how many of us have learned, to our chagrin, that our lives seem to be always getting busier? Delaying Torah study won't lead to future learning, but to no learning at all.

A dear friend, Allen Estrin, realized one day that his long-standing plans to read through the Hebrew Bible in its entirety would never happen. And so, one morning, he read the first two chapters of the Torah's first book, Genesis. And then the next morning, he read the next two chapters. And the following morning, another two. The exercise occupied about fifteen minutes a day. Even when he had extra time, he didn't read additional chapters (in such instances, he would study the two chapters in greater depth), and even when he had little time he forced himself not to read less. He simply made a firm determination never to miss the reading of the two chapters. He continued on his program for approximately 460 days, until he completed the Hebrew Bible in its entirety, from Genesis through the second book of Chronicles.

Though Hillel devoted himself to extensive daily study, and during his early, poor days did so only after first spending many hours in physical labor, he did not impose such demands on everyone else. He just urged people not to cite their crowded schedules as an excuse not to study at all, and exhorted them not to delude themselves into thinking that what they don't have time for now, they will have time for in the future. People who begin a course of study now will develop the self-discipline necessary to keep studying for the rest of their lives. People who delay will find, as Hillel predicted, that they "never have free time."*

So what about us, twenty-first-century disciples of Hillel? When should we start with some daily study? Perhaps we are best guided by the famous question Hillel posed as a capstone to the two challenges about being for oneself and being for others: "If not now, when?"

The first two chapters of Genesis is not a bad place to start.

---

* Hillel, *Ethics of the Fathers* 2:4.

17

"If I Am Not for Myself, Who Will Be for Me? And If I Am [Only] for Myself, What Am I?": Passionate Moderation

In this statement, Hillel poses two questions, each intended to articulate a paradox.* The first challenges an attitude of absolute altruism pursued at the expense of one's own interests. As Hillel suggests, if a person is not concerned with his own needs and well-being, why should he expect others to be? For example, if a sick person makes no effort to treat his illness, is it reasonable to expect others to devote themselves to doing so?

Such a level of self-sacrifice seems pointless. After all, the biblical verse that explicitly mandates, "Love your neighbor as yourself," implicitly commands us to love ourselves as well. Hillel was fully capable of preaching and practicing a radical love of others—for example, acting as a servant to a formerly rich man who felt bereft by having no one to serve

---

* Hillel, *Ethics of the Fathers* 1:14.

him (see p. 67)—without diminishing the sense of love for himself. In a world that generally assigned little value to hygiene, Hillel enjoyed bathing, an activity the rabbis regarded as somewhat luxurious, and therefore forbidden, for example, to mourners. Hillel, however, clearly regarded taking care of himself as both necessary and enjoyable.

On the other hand, "If I am only for myself, what am I?" This sentence should logically read, "*who* am I?" But, as Professor Louis Kaplan taught: "If you are only for yourself, you cease to be a real human being, and you become no longer a who, but a what."

In the popular mind, Darwin's notion of the "survival of the fittest" causes many people to see the world as a place in which people struggle not just with the elements, but also with one another. Which people will survive? Those who are best able to adapt to change, and those whose efforts at survival will not be hampered by extending undo attention and resources to their less capable brethren. The nineteenth-century Russian naturalist Pyotr Kropotkin was critical of Darwin's assumption that life is a constant struggle over limited food and space, in which there always have to be winners and losers. The lesson Kropotkin extracted from nature was not that people had to compete against one another for limited rewards, but that people did better when they cooperated with one another in a struggle against a harsh environment. Rabbi Harold Kushner has commented, "Yes, only the fittest survive, but the fittest are the ones best able to cooperate with their neighbors, to engage in mutual protection and helpfulness, not the strong ones who can overpower the weak and leave themselves with few friends and allies to help them through the winter."

I have found that, depending on the position they wish to argue, people often quote only a part of Hillel's words, and thereby corrupt his teaching. Some years ago, when I was writing an ethics advice column, a reader sent me the following question: "There's a famous teaching in the talmudic book, *Ethics of the Fathers*, 'If I am not for myself, who will be for me?' In line with this dictum, I give all my charity to Jewish causes; after all, if Jews don't support Jewish charitable needs, who will? My wife thinks I'm wrong, that I owe it to the society in which I live to spread around my giving. But I don't think there's anything wrong with what I am doing. Is there?"

I noted in my response that my questioner was only

quoting the first part of the talmudic citation, which then continues, "But if I am only for myself, what am I?" Just as it's wrong to ignore the Jewish community's needs, so, too, is it wrong to ignore the broader community of which we are also a part. And, it's not always easy to determine what is Jewish charitable giving and what isn't. Is finding a cure for cancer, for example, a non-Jewish issue, and supporting a Jewish school a Jewish one? Or are they both issues of concern to the Jewish community and therefore both causes you should support? Perhaps you are not aware that the Talmud— the very religious source on which you base your decision to support only Jewish causes—mandates that

"We provide financial support to the Gentile poor along with the Jewish poor" (*Gittin* 61a).

Because Jews comprise a little less than 2 percent of the American population, I think it is appropriate for them to give a disproportionate percentage of their charity to causes that serve their community, both because such causes matter so much to them and because their community depends on its members for support. It is fair to say, in line with Hillel, that if Jews don't support Jewish causes, who will?

But, as I wrote that questioner, "Don't give all your donations to your own community. It's not good for your character. If you do that long enough, you'll stop seeing everyone as being equally created in God's image and therefore worthy of your help. We are, after all, all members of one race, the human race."

This is exactly, I believe, what Hillel wished to convey. In your personal life, you should not veer off to an extreme, treating yourself as a nonentity and only others as important. You have the right to fight for and to push yourself forward. Be for yourself. Just don't be only for yourself.

Final Thoughts:
Why We Need Hillel
Now More Than Ever

Has Hillel been ignored? On first reading, the question seems ridiculous. Hillel is probably the Talmud's best-known rabbi, and even people with meager levels of Jewish knowledge are apt to be familiar with the story of his teaching the essence of Judaism to a non-Jew who was standing on one foot.

But the fact that a story is well known does not mean that its message is remembered. What, after all, was it that Hillel told the non-Jew: "What is hateful unto you, do not do unto your neighbor. This is the whole Torah, all the rest is commentary. Now, go and study."

The core teachings of Judaism, in Hillel's explanation, are to act ethically and to keep learning. Implicit in this formulation is the idea that while faith and religion matter greatly—Hillel meticulously observed the Jewish rituals governing the laws between people and God— but that they need not be the starting point of a religious journey. The fact that Hillel subsumes God and ritual observance under "commentary" is not the same as a modern scholar calling them "footnotes." Commentary matters a great deal. Still, there is no getting around the simplicity of Hillel's teaching, which lays an ethical cornerstone for an entire religious edifice. One might have thought that if Judaism's preeminent figure presented this summation of Judaism in so forceful a manner, it would permanently influence how Jews understand Jewish religiosity.

But has it? To this day, if two Jews are speaking about a third, and one of them asks if the person being discussed is religious, the answer is invariably based on the person's level of ritual, not ethical, observance. "He keeps kosher, he keeps Shabbat; yes, he is religious," or "She doesn't keep kosher, she doesn't keep Shabbat; no, she's not religious." It is virtually inconceivable that you would overhear the following conversation:

"Is so-and-so religious?"
"Oh, definitely."
"How do you know?"
"Because he's very careful never to embarrass anyone, particularly in public. And he always judges other people fairly."

Conversations such as this simply don't happen. Religiosity today—and perhaps even during Hillel's time—is assessed on the basis of ritual observance. If a Jew is known not to observe Shabbat or kashrut, that individual is regarded as nonreligious, even if his or her ethical behavior is exemplary and is based on what the ethics of the Torah and Talmud demand of him. In such a case, people might say, "Unfortunately, he is not religious, but he's a wonderful person." On the other hand, if a person keeps Shabbat and kashrut, but violates, for example, Jewish laws on business ethics or, in violation of the Torah, speaks unfairly and inappropriately of others, it wouldn't occur to people to say that such a person is not religious. Rather, they might say, "He's religious, but unfortunately he's not ethical."

It is inconceivable that Hillel would have described a person who consistently violates Judaism's fundamental ethical laws (obviously, no one's observance is perfect) as a "religious" Jew. Yet somehow, his teaching to the non-Jew has become a sort of nostrum; nice but largely empty words that have little to do with reality. The Talmud might have favored Hillel's response, but in Jewish life one wonders if it has ever been taken seriously. I believe this reality is to the great detriment of the Jewish people. The time has come not just to quote Hillel's words to the non-Jew, but to actually take them seriously.

It is worth recalling that the story of Hillel's summary statement of Judaism occurs in the context of three encounters between Hillel and non-Jews interested in converting to Judaism. The non-Jews all set up unusual conditions for becoming Jewish. One will convert on condition that Hillel teaches him the essence of Judaism in the briefest of summaries. A second will convert on condition that he be bound solely by the laws of the Written Torah, and not the Oral Law, which represents the rabbinical understanding of Torah law. The third will convert on condition that he be appointed High Priest, a request both arrogant and in direct violation of Torah law.*

All three Gentiles first approach Shammai; two of them are chased away with a stick, and the third with an insult. Hillel's response? Acceptance. In addition to converting the man who requests the short summary of Judaism, he also converts the two men with the even more peculiar demands, and then sets about showing them the unreasonableness of their requests. He leads one to understand why an Oral Law is necessary, and leads the second to understand why he can't be a priest of any sort, let alone a High Priest. Hillel's confidence in Judaism is such that he sincerely believes that once they convert, they will continue to grow in their Jewishness. In the meantime, whatever they are observing will be more beneficial than if they do not convert and observe nothing at all.

The Talmud clearly regards Hillel's approach to the converts as superior to that of Shammai. It records an encounter in which the three men get together and conclude: "Shammai's great impatience sought to drive us from the world, but Hillel's gentleness brought us under the wings of the Divine Presence" (*Shabbat* 31a).

Based on this behavior of the Talmud's preeminent sage, would it not be fair to reach the following conclusions:

• Hillel is open and encouraging to non-Jews who wish to become Jews;

• Hillel favors converting people quickly rather than slowly

---

* Priesthood is hereditary and transmitted through the paternal line. Therefore, a person whose father is not a priest cannot be a priest either.

and focusing on their Jewish education subsequent to the conversion (in addition, as a condition of conversion, many contemporary rabbis insist that converts commit to providing their children with an intensive Jewish education);

- Hillel does not insist on a commitment by a convert, prior to conversion, to *fully* observe Jewish law, a commitment that we have learned—from the American-Jewish experience—few converts are prepared to make in advance.

Based on these three anecdotes about Hillel, all of the conclusions make logical sense, but they have nothing to do with how Jewish law and life has developed. In the traditional Jewish community, the long-standing policy has been to discourage converts, insist on a long, sometimes years-long, period of study, and demand, in advance of conversion, a commitment to *full* observance of all Jewish laws. I cited earlier the rabbinic scholar at a leading Orthodox seminary who told rabbinical students never to convert a non-Jew unless they were willing to bet $100,000 of their own money that the convert would observe all Jewish laws.

In other words, Hillel's policy concerning converts is spoken of very approvingly in the Talmud, while Shammai's policy of distancing himself from would-be converts comes closer to how Jewish life has so often been lived.*

Here, too, the time has come to take Hillel as he meant himself to be taken: seriously. If non-Jews come knocking at a Jewish door, they should be made to feel welcome. Their

* Though without being as insulting as Shammai was.

questions should be answered. It is unlikely Jews would, under any circumstances, drive them off with a stick, but unsympathetic words might be almost as discouraging and painful. And certainly if they express interest in becoming Jewish, they should be treated with interest and encouragement. Hillel understood this.

In the realm of education, Hillel opposed the employment of hot-tempered teachers, arguing that "the highly impatient person cannot teach" (*Ethics of the Fathers* 2:5). Yet the history of Jewish education is filled with hot-tempered teachers.

Here as well, Hillel must be our guide. As important as it is that a teacher know the material he is teaching, it is even more important that he love the material and love the students whom he is teaching. A Talmudic passage teaches, "A person learns Torah only from a place that his heart wants" (*Avodah Zarah* 19a). And, as Hillel used to say, "To the place that I love, there my feet lead me" (*Sukkah* 53a).

Only people filled with a sense of ethical obligation and imbued with the rabbinic teaching, "Let the honor of your students be as dear to you as your own" (*Ethics of the Fathers* 4:12), are fit to teach a religion whose essence is ethical obligation and the Golden Rule. The Shammaite model—not admitting those of undistinguished background, those who are poor and those who do not possess wisdom—does not work, certainly not for the masses of people today who know nothing of Judaism, and whom a Shammaite philosophy has written off. That is why the Talmud cites the conclusion of the three converts, that the impatience of Shammai would have driven them away from God, but Hillel's gentleness brought them near. We ignore Hillel's advice about ill-tempered people, and those who drive off others instead of drawing them near, at our peril.*

Hillel also displayed enormous legislative courage and legal creativity. When the compassionate Torah law canceling debts in a recurrent seven-year cycle caused lenders to stop extending loans to the poor, Hillel enacted a new category of legislation, the *prozbol*, based on a new concept of legislation called *tikkun olam* ("bettering the world"), which enabled him to modify a number of Torah laws that were in effect undermining Torah ethics (see pp. 47–48). This, too, is an aspect of Hillel that has too often been ignored. To cite just one example: Jewish laws mandating kosher slaughter were obviously intended to minimize the pain caused to animals; they form part of a whole set of biblical laws concerned with the kindly treatment of animals.[1]

Why is it, then, that despite all the publicity given to the cruel treatment of newborn calves† (read the footnote below

---

* An infrequently quoted Talmudic passage teaches that Timna, a female character in the book of Genesis, came from a royal non-Israelite household. At an early age, she became interested in the Israelite faith and sought to convert. But when she approached the patriarchs—at one time or another, all three of them—they did not accept her as a convert (the Talmud does not explain why). After this rebuff, Timna became the concubine of Eliphaz, the son of Esau, and gave birth to Amalek (Gen. 36:12). The nation that descended from Amalek (also known as Amalek) subsequently became the most hated enemy of the ancient Israelites (Exod. 17:8–16). But all this did not have to happen. As the rabbis conclude: "[The Patriarchs] should not have rejected Timna" (*Sanhedrin* 99b).

† A description of a visit to a dairy farm in 2000 conveys the following por-

if you have the stomach for it), we still find such meat (veal) widely available for sale at kosher butchers?* It is permitted to be eaten because technically the veal calves are slaughtered according to the laws of kosher slaughter, which are intended, certainly in part, to minimize an animal's pain. But can veal eaters, once they become aware of how calves are treated, be confident that God will say to them, "Enjoy your meat. I really don't care how veal calves are treated during their lifetime, as long as they are slaughtered in the proper manner when killed." The case against veal is so self-evident that one would love to see a simple ruling along the

———

trait of the treatment of newborn calves. The calves are generally raised in a bare wooden crate that is too narrow for them to turn around in. They are put on diets that are very low in iron, so that the calves' flesh "instead of becoming the normal healthy red color of a 16-week-old calf on pasture, will retain the pale pink color and soft texture of 'prime veal.'" They are also denied hay or straw for bedding because the calf will eat it out of its desire for roughage, and the iron the straw contains will change the color of the calf's flesh. The stall in which the calf is confined is wooden for the same reason. If it would have an iron fitting, the calf would lick it. For the same reason, the crate is too small to allow the calf to turn around. If it could, then the calf, out of its craving for iron, would lick its own urine (Peter Singer and Jim Mason, *The Ethics of What We Eat* (New York: Holtzbrinck, 2006, pp. 58–59). In some farms, the calves are kept in darkness for up to twenty-three hours a day. More often than not, the individual cages in which the animals are held "prevent . . . the animals from having any contact with other calves, even preventing them from seeing another calf, causing unreasonable social isolation." (Most of the material in this note is drawn from Rabbi Pamela Barmash, unpublished 2007 responsa on "Veal Calves" for the Rabbinical Assembly Committee on Jewish Law and Standards.)

* Obviously, I am upset that veal is available at nonkosher butchers as well, but I expect Jewish law's ethical teachings to have their first and primary impact on Jews.

lines of Hillel: "*Mipnei tikkun olam* (for the betterment of the world), the sale and consumption of veal is forbidden because continuing to allow such food to be eaten causes immense suffering to animals."

These four brief examples—

- insisting that ethics is the essence of Jewish religiosity
- maintaining an openness and receptivity to non-Jews who wish to convert
- advancing the exclusion of mean-tempered, volatile, and verbally abusive people from the teaching profession
- utilizing the notion of *tikkun olam* to root out any unfairness or unintended cruelty in Jewish law

document just how much Hillel still has to teach us, even two thousand years after his death.

There are few Jews for whom Hillel's teachings are not instructive. He is a vital force for those secular Jews who should know that some of the values most dear and fundamental to many of them flow from religious tradition. For those Jews who are suspicious of *tikkun olam* as an operating philosophy of Judaism, Hillel offers an affirmation that ethics is not a modern-day politically correct dilution, but an abiding, central principle in Judaism. To those Jews who define themselves by the notion of *tikkun olan*, Hillel also insists upon Torah study and attention to both ritual and law. And for those who do study and who scrupulously observe Jewish law, Hillel can inspire a radical revision of religion by defining the essence of religiosity as "What is hateful unto you, do not do unto your neighbor." By accepting this definition, we can put an end to the centuries-old caricature of Judaism that defines religiosity by ritual observance alone. In doing so, and we have done so for far too long, Judaism has ceded to Christianity those elements—love and inclusiveness—that are central teachings of Judaism. Hillel reminds us that it isn't a "they have this, but we have that" situation. The principles and behavior the world associates with Jesus—the supreme significance of loving behavior, the confidence to coin concise epigrams and to extract an essence, the openness to others—predate Jesus in the person of the Talmud's greatest rabbinic figure, Hillel.

And, finally, for those non-Jews who see Judaism as a closed book, and the Jewish people as "a nation that dwells alone" and that wishes to dwell alone, Hillel offers an invitation to open, to enter, and to study.

Hillel has long been the Talmud's most famous rabbi. The time has now come to let him become its most influential.

For Those Who Oppose Converting People Without a Prior Commitment to Full Observance of Jewish Law

This does not mean that we should not forge a commitment by the convert to some level of observance, we just need I believe a more liberal standard than some contemporary rabbis insist upon. In the ritual realm, for example, it is obviously important that would-be converts be taught the laws of Shabbat, kashrut, and the holidays, and the significance and benefit of practicing these laws. The approach I am advocating is consistent, I believe, not only with Hillel's teachings but also with that of the late Sephardic chief rabbi of Israel, Ben-Zion Uziel (1880–1953), who argued for a policy of greater openness to potential converts. In *Piskei Uziel*, one of his volumes of responsa (see number 65), he considers a question posed to him by a rabbi outside of Israel. The questioner notes the large increase in the number of Jewish men marrying non-Jewish women, and writes that some of the men desire their family members to become Jews. They have approached local rabbis with the request that their wives and children be converted. He asks whether such conversions should be performed, because these men do not properly observe the Sabbath and Jewish holidays, and disregard the kashrut regulations. As another rabbi, facing the same situation, expressed it: "May we convert the non-Jewish wife and children of a Jewish man when we know that he is not observant and does not intend to have his family observe the commandments?"

While immersion in a *mikvah* and circumcision for males are absolute prerequisites for conversion, Rabbi Uziel insists that the same cannot be said regarding a commitment to observing all the commandments. He cites the sixteenth-century code of Jewish law, the *Shulchan Arukh*, which rules that a rabbinical court should acquaint a non-Jew who comes to convert with the principles of the faith (for example, the oneness of God) "in great detail," whereas, regarding the commandments, the would-be convert should "be told about some of the less weighty and some of the more weighty commandments. . . .* This, however, should not be carried to excess nor to too great detail" (*Yoreh De'ah* 268:2). Based on his understanding of this passage, Rabbi Uziel concludes: "From here it can be explicitly derived that we do not demand that the would-be convert observe the commandments, nor is the *bet din* (the Jewish court) required to be certain that he will observe them." Furthermore, if a Jewish court converts someone without teaching him the commandments, traditional Jewish law deems the conversion valid (which would not be the case, for example, if a Jewish court performed a conversion without the convert's immersing in a *mikvah*). Therefore, we may conclude that a commitment to "observing the commandments is not a necessary condition for conversion" and that these women and children can and should be converted.

Rabbi Uziel goes on to express the hope that these converts will eventually come to observe the commandments (*mitzvot*). Until then, as I understand it, we may regard observance of the commandments the converts likely will keep (for example, observing Yom Kippur and giving charity) as so significant that it is well worth granting them this opportunity. What distinguishes such an approach is the focus on the merit of those commandments that the convert will observe rather than the ritual violations the convert will commit.

One final point: regarding those who oppose converting

---

* And informal, for example, that violation of the Sabbath is a serious offense.

people who are not likely to be fully observant, Rabbi Uziel declares, "In this generation, shutting the door in the face of converts is a weighty and grievous matter. For it opens the gates wide and pushes Israelite men and women toward converting [to another religion] and exiting from the community of Israel [*k'lal Yisrael*] or toward assimilating among gentiles." While many Orthodox rabbis regard with distaste those who wish to convert without becoming fully observant, contemporary rabbi Marc Angel regards their mind-set far more sympathetically: "They do not want to reject the Torah but want to be included in the Jewish community."*

---

* "Another Halakhic Approach to Conversion," in Emanuel Feldman and Joel B. Wolowelsky, eds., *The Conversion Crisis*, p. 55.

APPENDIX 1

"He Who Does Not Increase, Will Decrease": Additional Teachings of Hillel

Do not separate yourself from the community.
—HILLEL, *Ethics of the Fathers* 2:5

In the Torah's opening chapter, God announces six times concerning His creation, "And the Lord saw that it was good." The first thing God declares not good is aloneness: "It is not good for man to be alone" (Gen. 2:18). Because this passage is speaking in the context of the creation of Eve, people assume the verse is simply directed to marital happiness; it is not good for a man to be without a wife, or for a woman to be without a husband.

But the verse has far broader implications. It is not healthy for people to segregate themselves from their community, and it is also not right. It is particularly important not to do so when your community needs you. In the biblical book of Esther, Mordechai sends a message to Queen Esther, instructing her to intervene with her husband, King Ahasuerus, to cancel the order of destruction he has issued against the Jews at the behest of his adviser, Haman. The queen, who until now has kept her religious identity a secret, informs Mordechai that she can't intervene because approaching the king without having been summoned will put her at grave, possibly life-threatening, risk. In response, Mordechai warns her: "Do not imagine that you, of all the Jews, will escape with your life by being in the king's palace. On the contrary, if you keep silent in this crisis, relief and deliverance will come to the Jews from another quarter, while you and your father's house will perish. And who knows, perhaps you have attained royal position for just such a crisis?" (Esther 4:12–14). Esther does of course intervene and saves her people.

Moses is an earlier example of a Jew who takes upon himself his community's pain. Like Esther, he, too, could have remained in the king's palace and concealed his Israelite origins. Yet, "he went out to his kinfolk and witnessed their labors." When he saw an Egyptian overseer beating a Hebrew slave, he struck the overseer down (Exod. 2:11–12). This is one of only three incidents recorded in the Bible about Moses' life prior to his being chosen by God to lead the Israelites out of Egyptian slavery.

In line with Hillel's directive, the Talmud insists that Jews regard themselves as part of something bigger than their own lives: "When the community is in trouble, a person should not say, 'I will go to my house and I will eat and drink and be at peace with myself' " (*Ta'anit* 11a). Rabbi Berel Wein recalls that during World War II, his grandfather Rabbi Chayyim Zvi Rubenstein contracted to have his house in Chicago painted. But shortly before the work began, Rabbi Rubenstein received a letter describing the horrible sufferings being inflicted by the Nazis on the Jews in Europe (herding Jews into work camps, ghettos, and worse). Rabbi Rubenstein immediately called up the painter, assured the man that he would pay him, but canceled the paint job. As he explained to his wife, *"Ken men machen shein a haus ver yidden in der velt hoben azoi fil yesurim?"* ("Can one beautify his house when Jews elsewhere in the world have so much suffering?").[1]

This teaching applies as well to less extreme situations. As a general rule, Hillel wanted people to be at one with those around them: "Do not weep among those who are laughing, or laugh among those who are weeping. . . . The rule is, do not deviate from those around you" (*Derekh Eretz Zuta* 5:5).

Hyam Maccoby notes that Hillel's teaching is a safeguard against selfishness, arrogance, and ingratitude: "Do not prize your own worth so much that you despise the community and withdraw from it, failing to realize how much you owe to it."[2]

He who does not increase, will decrease.
—HILLEL, *Ethics of the Fathers* 1:13

There is no comparison between one who reviews his studies 100 times, and one who reviews it 101 times.
—HILLEL, Chagigah 9a

Think of tests you took in high school on which you might have scored 90 or higher. If you were suddenly asked to take those same tests now, how would you perform? Most likely, a lot worse, because it is natural for people to forget much of what they have learned, certainly material learned many years ago.

The only way to continue growing in knowledge is through ongoing study. When you acquire new information, your knowledge expands and your wisdom grows. But if you don't continue learning and reviewing, your knowledge level will obviously decline, because you will not be adding new information and you will start to forget that which you once knew. As regards the second teaching, that you can't compare one who has reviewed his studies 100 times with one who has reviewed it 101 times, Hillel obviously believed that we need ongoing repetition to ensure that material already learned will not be forgotten.

I remember reading once of a world-renowned pianist who, long after he had achieved international renown, continued practicing seven or more hours a day. When a friend asked him why he didn't relax and take more time off, he answered, "If I miss a day of practice, I can feel the difference in my playing. If I miss a few days of practice, my manager will notice the difference. And if I miss a week of practice, everyone will notice."

Knowledge is not static. If you don't keep reviewing and adding, you decline. Which is why Hillel's advice to the would-be convert, "Go and study," applies to all of us, and at all times.

Eleven hundred years after Hillel, Maimonides responded to the question, "Until when is a person obligated to study Torah?" with the answer, "Until the day of one's death" ("Laws of Torah Study" 1:10).

> Because you drowned others, others drowned you; in the end, they that drowned you shall themselves be drowned.
>
> —HILLEL, *Ethics of the Fathers* 2:7

This was Hillel's comment on seeing a skull floating on the water's surface. If Hillel recognized the body in the water as being that of a violent person, his words are self-explanatory: "You practiced violence, and eventually the violence you directed against others was turned against you."[1] The problem is that the text provides no context. If we assume that Hillel did *not* know the identity of the corpse to whom he addressed his words, then we can choose to see this teaching as a statement of faith, specifically Hillel's faith in God's justice. God would not allow someone to arbitrarily be drowned; therefore we must assume that the person suffering such a fate is being justly punished.

The problem of course is that such certainty seems simpleminded, and even mean-spirited—simpleminded because one does not need to have the intellectual capabilities of a Hillel to know that there are people who die violently who did not lead lives of violence, and mean-spirited because it seems cruel to blame a person whom one does not know and about whom one knows nothing of his or her own violent death. It is one thing to say, "He got what he deserves" of someone whom we know for a certainty did great evil, quite another to say it of someone whom we don't know at all.

And so, I believe, we can only assume that Hillel *did* recognize the dead person and knew him to be a person of violence. That justice prevailed in such a circumstance would be reassuring. Hillel lived at the time of the murderous King Herod, who employed vicious people to carry out his often malevolent orders. Indeed, we know that he had two assassins drown his brother-in-law, the High Priest (see p. 11). That one of these people might have suffered the fate he inflicted on another would be just.

This explanation might well be wrong, but so far I have found none other of this enigmatic passage that is consistent with Hillel's well-deserved reputation for love of humankind and for judging people fairly.

> He who has acquired for himself a knowledge of Torah has acquired for himself life in the world to come.
>
> —HILLEL, *Ethics of the Fathers* 2:8

Hillel is, it would seem, the first rabbinic sage to speak about an afterlife. The idea that the soul survives the death of the body is not explicitly stated in the Bible. The Torah cites God as exhorting the Israelites to follow His ways, to practice justice, and to obey His commandments. In

Deuteronomy, the Torah's final book, God warns the Israelites that if they worship other gods, He "will shut up the skies so that there will be no rain and the ground will not yield its produce, and you will soon perish from the good land that the Lord is assigning to you" (Deut. 11:17).

But one looks in the Torah in vain for verses explicitly saying something such as, "If you obey My laws, you will live in eternal bliss," or conversely, "If you disobey My laws, you will suffer punishment after you die."

How does one account for this silence about the afterlife?* I suspect there is a correlation between the Torah's non-discussion of this topic and the fact that the Torah was revealed shortly after the Israelite sojourn in Egypt. The Egyptian society in which the Israelite slaves dwelled was obsessed with death and the afterlife. The holiest Egyptian literary work was *The Book of the Dead*, and the major achievement of many pharaohs was the erection of giant tombs called pyramids. In contrast, the Torah is obsessed with this world, so much so that it forbids its priests *(kohanim)* from having contact with dead bodies (Lev. 21:1–2). The Torah, therefore, might be silent about the afterlife out of a desire to ensure that Judaism not evolve in the direction of the death-obsessed Egyptian religion. And it was not only the Egyptian religion that developed this obsession.

---

* One explicit mention of survival following death is in a later biblical book, 1 Samuel, chapter 28, in which the dead prophet Samuel appears in an angry vision—and one in which he speaks—to King Saul. But I have found that relatively little attention is paid to this episode in discussions of Jewish attitudes on the afterlife.

Throughout history, religions that assign a very important role to the afterlife often permit other religious values to become distorted. For example, it was belief in the afterlife that motivated the Spanish Inquisitors to torture human beings until they announced that they were accepting Christ. The Inquisitors believed that it was better to torture people for a few days in this world until they "acquired" right beliefs and thereby save them from the eternal torments of hell.[3] Unfortunately, the obsession with the afterlife continues to have awful moral consequences. Among extremist Islamists, "suicide bombers" are promised that in return for murdering innocent people whom the Islamists regard as enemies or heretics, they will immediately receive heavenly rewards, including the services of seventy-two virgins. In light of the evils to which an overconcern with the afterlife can lead, the Torah believed, I presume, that the task of getting its adherents focused on this world is preeminent.

But during Hillel's time, a period when there was much suffering in the Jewish world under the cruel hand of Herod, a suffering that later intensified under the oppressive rule of Rome, it became important to emphasize that Judaism does not believe that good people and evil people endure the same fate—nothingness—after they die. Hillel therefore enunciates the doctrine of a life beyond this life: acquire Torah, he promised people, and your life will be everlasting.

The influence of Hillel's words, and the consolation and inspiration they have offered ever since, have been profound. The doctrine of divine reward and punishment and the notion of an afterlife became the eleventh of Maimonides' Thirteen Principles of the Jewish faith. And throughout centuries of oppression and deprivation, the belief in an afterlife and the survival of the soul enabled countless Jews to confront their oppressors with the assurance that there was an existence beyond this one.

Hillel's Concern with Not Causing Suffering to Innocent People

Hillel's trust in his fellow Jews' common sense led him to overturn a ruling of his rabbinic colleagues that would have destroyed the lives of dozens, perhaps hundreds, of Jewish residents of Alexandria, Egypt.

The issue that prompted the crisis was Judaism's strict laws concerning the status of a married woman, and the point at which Jewish law defines a couple as married. Today, the Jewish wedding ceremony consists of two series of blessings, the *birkat erusin* (betrothal blessings) and the *birkat nisu'in* (wedding blessings). The rabbi recites the betrothal blessings, the groom places a ring on the bride's finger, the *ketubah* (marriage contract) is read, and then the seven wedding blessings are recited. The entire ceremony generally occurs in a span of fifteen to twenty minutes.[4]

In the Talmudic era, the procedure was altogether different. A man and a woman formally signified their intention to wed a full year before the wedding, in the ceremony known as *erusin*, betrothal. At that time, the *ketubah* was signed, the two *erusin* blessings were recited, and the couple became betrothed. They remained in the state of *erusin* for about a year, during which time the woman was expected to assemble her trousseau and prepare for marriage, while the man readied himself financially. Unlike modern engagements, the *erusin* was regarded as legally binding, and could be terminated only by divorce. During the year between the betrothal and the wedding ceremony, the man and woman were forbidden to have sexual relations, and the woman was, of course, forbidden to any other man as well.

A serious problem among the Alexandrian Jews was brought to Hillel's attention. It sometimes happened that a betrothed woman did not go through with the wedding ceremony, but instead married another man (the text speaks of another man running off with her) without first securing a divorce. In the absence of the divorce, the woman was still regarded as married to the man who betrothed her. Therefore, this new marriage was considered an act of adultery, and the children born from it were regarded as *mamzerim* (bastards), and forbidden by Torah law from marrying any Jew other than another *mamzer*. As if this was not bad enough, the stain of *mamzerut* was eternal, passed on from generation to generation.

The sages of the time (we are speaking of the late first century B.C.E.) were not pleased to impose the stigma of *mamzerut* on the couple's children, but there seemed no way out. Hillel, as in the case of the *prozbol*, wanted to find a legal basis for not enforcing a law that would inflict great misery, particularly on the couple's innocent children. The Talmud explains how Hillel proceeded:

"When the issue came before the court, Hillel the Elder said to these children, 'Bring me the *ketubah* of your mother.' They brought him the *ketubah* of their mother, and he found that it was written [in this *ketubah* and in all the Alexandrian *ketubot*] 'When you enter the chuppah [the wedding canopy], you will be to me a wife.' " This innovative language, distinctive to the *ketubot* written in Alexandria, meant that the community did not regard (as did the rest of the Jewish world) a woman who participated in the ceremony of *erusin* as married. Rather, marriage was effected and finalized only when the couple went under the marital canopy and the seven marriage blessings were recited. Though the Alexandrian Jews had acted on their own in inserting new language and conditions into the *ketubah*, Hillel ruled that its language was clear and should be obeyed. In consequence, Hillel was able to invalidate the original betrothal, thereby validating the new marriage and releasing the children of this marriage from the status of *mamzerut*. This ruling was accepted by all the other rabbis (*Bava Metzia* 104a). Later, in medieval times, Jewish law was amended so that the betrothal and wedding ceremonies were conducted at the same time—instead of a year apart—thereby avoiding the problems that could ensue if a couple, subsequent to the *erusin*, decided not to marry.

Understanding that following the strict letter of the law would impose an injustice, Hillel was able to avoid the harsh status of *mamzer*, which would have cut off such children and their descendants from the rest of the Jewish community forever.

The Talmud does not use the rationale of *tikkun olam*, bettering the world, to explain this ruling of Hillel, but obviously it is in line with the previous such rulings that he issued.

Ezra, Hillel, and Rabbi Chiyya: Salvation Comes from Babylonia

At first, when Torah was forgotten from Israel, Ezra came up from Babylonia and reestablished it. Again it was forgotten, and Hillel the Babylonian came and reestablished it. Again it was forgotten, and Rabbi Chiyya and his sons came and reestablished it.

—*Sukkah* 20a

The Land of Israel is of course the Jewish people's Holy Land, the country in which Jerusalem is located, where the Great Temples stood, and where the *Me'arat Ha-Machpelah*, the caves of the patriarchs and matriarchs, is located. But the Land of Israel is not the place where many of the greatest works of Jewish literature were written. The Bible itself records the giving of the Torah to Moses on Mount Sinai, outside Israel. Later, two editions of the Talmud were produced. The first, edited in Israel, is known as the Jerusalem Talmud. It occupies a distinguished place in Jewish life, but is certainly not comparable in significance to the Babylonian Talmud, compiled and edited in what is now known as Iraq.

The importance of the Diaspora is underscored in this Talmudic reminder that it was three Diaspora Jews, Ezra,

Hillel, and Rabbi Chiyya, who saved Judaism from oblivion. After the destruction of the First Temple by Nebuchadnezzar of Babylonia (586 B.C.E.) and the subsequent seventy-year exile, many laws were forgotten; Ezra came to Israel with the returning Jews and restored them. To cite just one example, the Bible records that the holiday of Sukkot, ordained in the Torah (see Lev. 23:42), had been totally forgotten, and was restored to observance by Ezra (Neh. 8:14–18).

During the time of the Second Temple, many other laws were forgotten, for example, the ruling as whether or not the Passover sacrifice overrides the Sabbath prohibition of slaughtering an animal (see p. 13). Hillel, who moved to Israel from Babylonia, is the one person who can teach the Bnai Beteira, the religious leadership, the correct thing to do.

The case of Rabbi Chiyya is less dramatic. He lived, after all, in the generation of Rabbi Judah the Prince, compiler and editor of the Mishnah (and a descendant of Hillel as well), so the situation could not have been as desperate as it was during the times of Ezra and Hillel. Nonetheless, *Bava Metzia* 85b demonstrates Rabbi Chiyya's considerable ingenuity in motivating and educating many new students. He would go to villages where there were no teachers, find five children and teach each of them one of the five books of the Torah. Then he would take six other students and teach each of them the six orders of the Mishnah. Then he would tell them, "During the time that I return to my place and come here again, teach Torah to one another and teach

Mishnah to one another." In this way, Rabbi Chiyya concluded, "I make sure that the Torah is never forgotten from the Jewish people."

A final thought. Though the subject of conversion to Judaism is not discussed extensively in the Talmud, all three of these figures had strongly demarcated views on this issue, the first negative and the latter two very positive. When Ezra moved to Israel, he confronted a Jewish community saturated with intermarriage, and he ordered Jewish men to end their relationships with their non-Jewish wives and to cast off the children born from these unions. No mention is made in the biblical book that bears his name of his raising the possibility of having the non-Jewish spouses and their children convert to Judaism.*

On the other hand, as is clear from the Talmudic passages cited earlier in this book, the other two figures credited with saving and restoring Jewish life in Israel were highly receptive to converts. Hillel converted three non-Jewish men who came to him with highly unusual conditions for becoming Jews, and Rabbi Chiyya converted a woman who had fallen in love with one of his students, and in love with Judaism as well.

---

* The Jewish historian Professor Shaye Cohen argues that there was no conversion process at the time. See his book *The Beginnings of Jewishness: Boundaries, Varieties, Uncertainties.*

A Final, Brief Teaching: Hillel, the Man of God

The Talmud reports that the rabbis were gathered in the house of Gurya in Jericho when a heavenly voice declared, " 'There is one among you who is worthy that the Divine Presence rest upon him, but his generation is not worthy.' They all looked upon Hillel. And when he died, they lamented him as a hasid [a pious person, a saint], and as an *anav* [a man of great humility]" (*Sotah* 48b).

Did this story happen exactly as this passage describes? Were the rabbis seated together, engaged in discussion when an unrecognized voice, whose source was divine, made this dramatic pronouncement? I don't know, but what I am sure of is that what the lawyer said to the judge about the Chafetz Chayyim—the story with which this book began—applies to Hillel as well. "They don't tell stories like that about you and me."

APPENDIX 2

Hillel's Seven *Middot* of Torah Interpretation

There are seven principles (*middot*) of interpretation by which Hillel explained and understood biblical law (the passage enumerating the seven principles is found in *The Fathers According to Rabbi Nathan*, 37:10).[1] Although these *middot* were not Hillel's innovations, he does seem to have been the first to crystallize and expound upon them. Later, Rabbi Yishmael (first–second century C.E.) enumerated thirteen rules by which the Torah is understood (which include all of Hillel's rules except for the sixth); his listing is recited daily in the *Shacharit* (morning) prayer service.

1. *Kal va-chomer:* a conclusion drawn from a lenient law that is then applied to a stricter one. The term may be translated, although not literally, as "how much more so." For example, if we know that a certain country mandates capital punishment for the crime of stealing, how much more so can we be sure that it mandates capital punishment for murder. To cite an example from Jewish ritual law: the laws of the Sabbath are stricter than the laws of the biblical festivals (holidays

such as Passover, Shavuot, and Sukkot). For example, it is forbidden to cook food on the Sabbath, but it is permitted to cook food on the festivals. We can therefore reason that if it is forbidden to pluck fruit from a tree on the festivals (a day when food may be cooked), how much more so can we be sure that it is forbidden to pluck fruit on the Sabbath.

2. *Gezerah shavah:* comparing similar words or expressions in different biblical verses, and understanding how they clarify one another. For example, Numbers 28:2 cites God's statement to Moses, "Command the Israelite people and say to them: 'Be punctilious in presenting to Me at its proper time (*be-mo'ado*) the offerings of food due Me.'" Jewish law understands the word *be-mo'ado* as meaning that the daily sacrifice must be brought even on the Sabbath (normally, the work involved in preparing and sacrificing an animal would be forbidden on the Sabbath). Since the same word, *be-mo'ado* is used in stating the law of the Passover sacrifice, "Let the Israelite people offer the Passover sacrifice *be-mo'ado*" (Num. 9:2), Jewish law understands this verse as meaning that the Passover sacrifice is offered even if its appointed day, the first night of Passover, falls on the Sabbath (see *Pesachim* 66a; the ruling that the Passover sacrifice must be brought on the Sabbath is the ruling that led to Hillel's appointment as *nasi*, or leader; see pp. 13–15).

3. *Binyan av:* a general principle (a sort of archetype) contained in one or two Torah laws that is applicable to all related laws. Deuteronomy 24:6 states that when a lender

makes a loan he cannot take as collateral "a handmill or an upper millstone," which are used to prepare flour for bread. Depriving the borrower of such utensils is forbidden "for that would be taking someone's life in collateral." Based on this, the rabbis conclude that "everything that is used for preparing food is forbidden to be taken as collateral, for that would be taking someone's life in collateral" (Mishnah *Bava Metzia* 9:13). A second example: in a society that permitted slavery, biblical law ruled that if a master "strikes the eye of his slave, male or female, and destroys it, he shall let him go free on account of his eye. If he knocks out the tooth of his slave, male or female, he shall let him go free on account of his tooth" (Exod. 21:26–27). From these two instances, the Talmud deduces that when any part of the slave's body that will not regenerate (for example, the tip of a finger) is mutilated, the slave must be set free (see *Kiddushin* 24a).

4. *Klal u-perat:* when a general biblical law is followed by specifications, only the specified laws apply. Thus, Leviticus 18:6 prohibits sexual intimacy with anyone to whom one is related. But this verse is followed by example after example of those with whom one is forbidden to be intimate. So, this biblical prohibition is understood as forbidding only those relationships that are specified. Relations that are not specified, such as marriage between first cousins, are therefore permitted and were in fact long common in Jewish life.

5. *Perat u-klal:* This is the opposite of the preceding principle. When a specific statement in the Bible is followed by a general statement, all that is implied in the generalization also applies to the specific statement. Deuteronomy 22:3 states that one who finds a missing donkey or a missing garment must return it to its owner. It then concludes with "so too shall you do with anything that your fellow man loses and you find." Although the first part of the verse specifies the return only of a lost donkey or garment, the verse's concluding words make it clear that a donkey and garment are cited only as examples, and that in actuality you are required to return any lost item that you find.

6. *Ka-yotzei bo mi-makom acher:* an inference drawn from [an analogous case] elsewhere.

7. *Davar ha-lomed mei-inyano:* the interpretation of a word or passage based on its context. While there are laws in the Torah prohibiting stealing (see, for example, Lev. 19:11, 13), the rabbis understand the prohibition "You shall not steal" in the Ten Commandments as referring specifically to kidnapping (the stealing of a human being) with the intention of selling the person into slavery. How did the rabbis derive this seemingly idiosyncratic understanding of the eighth commandment? The two prohibitions preceding "You shall not steal" are the sixth commandment, "You shall not murder," and the seventh, "You shall not commit adultery." Because both murder and adultery are capital offenses, the rabbis deduced that the prohibition here against stealing

must also involve a capital offense. The only act of stealing that is punished with death is kidnapping, specifically when done with the intention of selling the victim into slavery: "He who kidnaps a person, whether he has sold him or is still holding him, shall be put to death" (Exod. 21:16; see both *Sanhedrin* 86a and Rashi's commentary on Exod. 20:13).

APPENDIX 3

Hillel's Teachings in *Pirkei Avot* *(Ethics of the Fathers)*

Of the sixty-three short books, or tractates, that make up the Mishnah, sixty-two are legal texts. For example, *Berakhot*, the Mishnah's first tractate, delineates the laws concerning appropriate blessings for various occasions. As one would expect, *Shabbat* specifies the Sabbath laws, and *Sanhedrin*, the laws of the Jewish High Court. *Pirkei Avot* *(Ethics of the Fathers)* is the only one of the sixty-three tractates that does not deal with laws. Rather, it transmits the favorite moral advice, insights, and maxims of the leading rabbinic scholars of different generations (all of whom lived no later than 200 C.E., when the Mishnah was compiled).

Of the seventy-two scholars quoted in *Ethics of the Fathers*, Hillel is by far the most widely cited. His teachings appear in seven *mishnayot* (seven paragraphs of the Mishnah), while Rabbi Akiva, the second most frequently cited sage, appears in four. These favorite maxims of Hillel are—along with the story of the would-be convert who inquired about Judaism's essence—the teachings for which he remains most widely known.

1:12. Hillel and Shammai received [the tradition] from them [Shmaya and Avtalion]. Hillel says: "Be of the disciples of Aaron, loving peace and pursuing peace, loving people and drawing them near to Torah."

1:13. He used to say: "A name made great is a name destroyed. He who does not increase will decrease. He who does not learn is deserving of death. He who uses the crown [of Torah for personal gain] shall soon be gone."

1:14. He used to say: "If I am not for myself, who will be for me? And if I am [only] for myself, what am I? And if not now, when?"

2:4. Hillel says: "Do not separate yourself from the community. Do not be too sure of yourself until the day of your death. Do not judge your fellow until you are in his place. Say nothing that cannot be understood, because in the end it will be understood. And do not say, 'When I have [free] time, I will study,' lest you never have [free] time."

2:5. He used to say: "A boor does not fear sin; an ignorant person cannot be a saint; one who is bashful will never learn; the highly impatient person cannot teach; not all who steep themselves in business grow wise; and in a place where there are no men [willing to take action], try to be a man."

2:7. He used to say: "The more flesh [one acquires], the more worms [in the grave]. The more possessions, the more worries. The more wives, the more witchcraft.* The more servant girls, the more promiscuity. The more man-servants, the more theft. The more Torah, the more life. The more contemplation [alternatively, 'schooling'], the more wisdom. The more counsel, the more understanding. The more charity, the more peace. He who has acquired a good name, has acquired it for himself. He who has acquired for himself a knowledge of Torah, has acquired for himself life in the world to come."

4:7. Rabbi Tzadok said: ". . . Do not use [the Torah] as a crown for self-glorification, or as a spade with which to dig." Likewise Hillel used to say: "One who makes worldly use of the crown [of the Torah] shall fade away." From this you learn that one who seeks personal benefit from the words of the Torah risks destroying his life.

* It was assumed that the different wives would use witchcraft to try to secure for themselves a greater measure of their husband's love.

GLOSSARY

Antiochus Epiphanes: The villain of the Hanukkah story, Antiochus Epiphanes was part of the Seleucid dynasty, an empire based in Syria that ruled for 250 years. Antiochus Epiphanes ruled from 175 to 164 B.C.E. In 168 B.C.E., fearing that the Jews were rebelling against him while he was busy with a campaign in Egypt, he established harsh laws forbidding the practice of Judaism and forcing Hellenization and Greek religion on the Jewish population. These laws led to the successful Jewish revolt in 167 B.C.E., under the leadership of the Hasmonean priestly family.

Aramaic: A Semitic language, related to Hebrew and Arabic, that flourished in the Mesopotamian world in different forms from approximately 700 B.C.E. to the middle of the first millennium C.E. It is still spoken by small groups in Lebanon, Turkey, and Kurdistan. The language of the Talmud and of other important Jewish texts, Aramaic was the lingua franca of Jews in Greek and Roman times, and was used for rabbinic writings for many hundreds of years. The kaddish prayer is in Aramaic.

Ashkenazi: Originally referred to Jews from Germany; eventually generalized to all Jews from western, central, and eastern Europe.

Beit Hillel/Beit Shammai: Literally, "The House of Hillel" and "The House of Shammai." These names refer to the students and followers of Hillel and Shammai—those who studied with them directly and those who studied with succeeding generations of their students.

Bible: Judaism's Bible consists of the Torah, also known as the Five Books of Moses, or Pentateuch; the Nevi'im, or Prophets, which includes books of early Israelite history as well as the literature of the prophets; and the Ketuvim, or Writings, which includes later Israelite historical narratives as well as the Psalms, Job, Proverbs, and the five megillot (The Song of Songs, Ruth, Lamentations, Ecclesiastes, and Esther). In Hebrew the Bible is known as the TaNaKh, an acronym formed from the names of its three parts.

Chafetz Chayyim: The popularly used name for Rabbi Israel Meir Kagan (1838–1933), the founder and head of a famous yeshiva in Radin, Belarus, and the author of several very important works of Jewish law. His first book, *Chafetz Chayyim*, published in 1873, is a study of the laws regarding gossip, slander, and tale bearing. He is also the author of the *Mishnah Berurah*, a commentary on the first volume of the *Shulchan Arukh*, the *Orakh Chayyim*.

David: The second king of ancient Israel, and son-in-law and rival of King Saul. Chosen by the prophet Samuel to succeed Saul, David successfully ruled a united Israel and was a heroic warrior, a musician, and a poet traditionally credited with the authorship of the book of Psalms. A towering biblical figure of tremendous charm as well as some personal failings, he ruled ca. 1000 B.C.E. to 960 B.C.E.

Diaspora: The Jewish communities outside the Land of Israel.

Edom: A Gentile nation in the biblical era, said to be descendants of Esau (who was also called Edom, or Red). In rabbinic lore, Edom is the eternal antagonist of the Jews, associated with Rome and later, during periods of oppression, with Christianity.

The Fathers According to Rabbi Nathan: This rabbinic text is an elaboration of and commentary on the Mishnah tractate *Pirkei Avot (Ethics of the Fathers). The Fathers According to Rabbi Nathan* is probably a post-Talmudic text, from between the fifth and eighth centuries. It follows the structure of *Ethics of the Fathers* and includes similar material.

First Book of Maccabees: An account of the rise of Antiochus Epiphanes, the successful Hasmonean revolt against him that took place in the mid-second century B.C.E., and the first generations of Hasmonean rule. It survives in Greek translation, but scholars agree that it was written in Hebrew. It was not included in the TaNaKh, but is included in Christian bibles as part of the Apocrypha, along with several other volumes that also cover this period.

Glossary

Hellenism: The creative fusion of local and Greek culture (art, philosophy, literature, religion, etc.) that emerged in the territories first conquered by Alexander the Great in the late fourth century B.C.E. As Greek language and ideas spread throughout the eastern Mediterranean and western Asia, no people, including the Jews, was immune to its influence, though many resisted certain aspects of it, as the Jews, for example, resisted polytheism.

Herod: A wily and vicious Jewish leader of Idumean (Edomite) descent who took control of the kingdom of Judea in 37 B.C.E. with the help of the Roman army. Blood-thirsty but also highly effective, he employed terrible violence against rivals and imagined rivals, massacring even his own family members when he suspected them of disloyalty. He built a massive and beautiful expansion of the Temple in Jerusalem in an attempt to win Jewish support. He ruled until 4 B.C.E.

High Priest: In any given generation, the leader of the priests charged with the sacred duty of offering sacrifices to God. Aaron, Moses's brother, was the first High Priest; his descendants became the priestly caste. In the period when Jewish worship centered on the Temple in Jerusalem, the High Priest was a figure of great religious and political importance. Over time the position became politicized and debased, and various political rulers of Judea attempted to consolidate their rule by placing allies in this sacred role.

Holy of Holies: This originally referred to the central chamber in the portable Tabernacle used by the Children of

Israel during the forty years they spent in the desert. It was the most sacred room in the Tabernacle and later in the Temple in Jerusalem. Only the High Priest was permitted to enter the Holy of Holies, and only on Yom Kippur, the Day of Atonement.

John Hyrcanus: Hasmonean ruler of Judea from 135 to 104 B.C.E. who forcibly converted the Idumeans to Judaism.

Karet: A Hebrew word meaning "to cut off" or "to be destroyed." A severe punishment that is biblically ordained for thirty-six specific transgressions, it is manifested as premature death and can be carried out only by God.

Maccabees: The Maccabees (also known as the Hasmoneans), were a priestly family who led the Judean revolt against Antiochus Epiphanes starting in 167 B.C.E. After the patriarch Mattathias's death at the start of the revolt, his son Judah assumed leadership. In 164 B.C.E Judah successfully wrested Jerusalem from the Seleucids and rededicated the Temple. Family members continued to rule Judea, eventually assuming the mantles of both kingship and high priesthood, and extended their territory through conquest and forced conversion. But battles among themselves and with opponents escalated into a civil war in 63 B.C.E that resulted in Roman intervention and brought the Hasmonean dynasty to an end.

Maimonides: Born in 1138 in Córdoba, Spain, Rabbi Moses

ben Maimon, also known as Rambam (an acronym of his Hebrew name), was the premier rabbinic authority of his time and a towering figure in Jewish history. A codifier of Jewish law, student of Greek and Arabic philosophy, and royal physician, he wrote seminal books of Jewish law, philosophy, and commentary. His Thirteen Principles of Faith, which were written as part of his Commentary on the Mishnah (completed in 1168), include belief in the existence and singular unity of God, the eternity of Torah, reward and punishment, the coming of the Messiah, and the resurrection of the dead.

Mezuzah: A parchment scroll on which verses from chapters 6 and 11 in Deuteronomy are written. The scroll is rolled up and placed inside a case that is affixed to the entry doorposts of Jewish homes, as well as to the doorposts of some interior rooms, as commanded in Deuteronomy 6:9 and 11:20.

Mikvah: Ritual bath. In the time of the Temple, the *mikvah* was used by priests and all those bringing sacrifices. Since the Temple's destruction in 70 C.E., the *mikvah* continues to be used by women after their menstrual cycles, by both men and women as part of the conversion process, and by some Jewish men before the Sabbath and certain holidays.

Mitzvot (singular, mitzvah): Commandments. According to Jewish tradition, there are 613 *mitzvot* listed in the Pentateuch. Colloquially, the word "mitzvah" is often used to mean "a good deed."

Mussaf: Hebrew for "add on." Originally the name for the additional sacrifice offered in the Temple on the Sabbath and holidays. After the destruction of the Temple, prayer services replaced the sacrifices, and *Mussaf* was the name given to the additional prayer service established for the Sabbath and holidays.

Nasi: "President" in modern Hebrew. The meaning of the word evolved from "important person" or "tribal chief" in the Bible. In the rabbinic period it referred to the leader of the Sanhedrin, a person who often also had significant power. For several centuries in Palestine, the *nasi* was from the family of Hillel.

Oral Torah: A term used for the corpus of rabbinic Jewish texts, especially the Mishnah and the Gemara, that explain and expand upon the commandments in the Torah. The Oral Law is traditionally believed to have been transmitted orally from God to Moses at Sinai, and thence through generations of leaders until it was written down between the third and sixth centuries C.E.

Pharisees: One of several Jewish groups vying for power and influence in the late Second Temple period. The Pharisees believed in the role of the Oral Law to explicate the Torah, and that the Oral Law empowered them to make emendations to Jewish law when necessary and to apply it to new situations. Contemporary Jews are heirs to the pharisaic traditions.

Pirkei Avot: The *Ethics of the Fathers.* One of the sixty-three tractates of the Mishnah, *Pirkei Avot* is a collection of ethical teachings attributed to generations of scholars who lived in the centuries just before and after the Common Era.

Responsa: The term for the continually evolving body of Jewish legal decisions developed as responses to questions posed to rabbis.

Sanhedrin: The "high court" in Jewish law. The Great Sanhedrin in Jerusalem, which was the ultimate authority in all matters of Jewish law, had seventy-one members. After the destruction of the Second Temple, the Sanhedrin was reconvened in the city of Yavneh, in northern Israel, and then in various other cities in the Galilee. It disbanded around 425 C.E.

Seder: From the Hebrew word for "order," the seder is the ritual meal on the first night (in the Diaspora, the first and second nights) of Passover, at which the story of the Exodus is retold and ritual foods eaten.

Sephardi: From the Hebrew word for Spain, and referring to the rites and practices of Jews descended from the exiled communities of Spain and Portugal. Colloquially, it is sometimes used to refer to any non-Ashkenazic Jews, although Jews from the Middle East are more accurately referred to as *eidot ha-mizrach*, or Oriental communities.

Shema: An affirmation of faith in the one God, and one of the core prayers of the Jewish liturgy. It begins with Deuteronomy 6:4, "Hear O Israel, the Lord Our God, the Lord is one," and continues through Deuteronomy 6:9

and with passages from Deuteronomy 11 and Numbers 15. The word "shema" means "hear" or "listen."

Shulchan Arukh: Literally, "the set table." This comprehensive, four-volume code of Jewish law completed in 1555 by the Sephardic rabbi Joseph Caro, and expanded shortly thereafter to include in italics Ashkenazic practice by Rabbi Moses Isserles, remains the authoritative legal code for observant Jews.

Spanish Inquisition: Beginning in 1481 and not officially abolished until 1808, the Inquisition was an office of the Catholic Church in Spain dedicated to rooting out false Christians, including Jews who had outwardly converted to Christianity but continued secretly to observe Jewish law and rituals. The Inquisition routinely tortured those who came under suspicion in order to get them to confess and name other false Christians. Those who were convicted of being false Christians were burned at the stake.

Tahor: A term that indicates one's positive status in matters of ritual purity. In the time of the Temple, only a person who was *tahor* could enter the Temple and participate in its rituals.

Talmud: From the Hebrew word for learn, and also known as the Oral Torah, the Talmud consists of collected oral teachings, commentaries, and anecdotes from the rabbis through the fifth century. The Talmud comprises the Mishnah, the teachings and commentaries collected and set down ca. 200 C.E. by Rabbi Judah the Prince, and the Gemara, rabbinic interpretations of the Mishnah developed from the third through fifth centuries and set down in the sixth century. Rabbinic academies in Babylonia and in Jerusalem each developed their own Talmud; the Babylonian version is more extensive and more definitive. Along with the Torah, the central text of Jewish law, the Talmud is printed on pages surrounded by medieval-era commentaries on its text.

Tamei: A term that indicates one's negative status in matters of ritual purity. In the time of the Temple, one who was *tamei* could not enter the Temple or participate in its rituals. Ways of becoming *tamei* included, most commonly, contact with a dead body and a woman undergoing her menstrual period. To regain *tahor* status, one would immerse in the *mikvah* and, in certain situations, bring an offering to the Temple.

Tefillin: Phylacteries. Small leather boxes, one going on the forehead and the other on the arm, worn by Jews during weekday morning prayers. Inside the boxes are parchment scrolls on which are written the four biblical texts that outline the commandment for wearing tefillin.

Temple: The Temple in Jerusalem was the central site of Jewish sacrificial worship in ancient Israel as well as the major national gathering place. The First Temple was built by King Solomon in the tenth century B.C.E. and survived for approximately four hundred years, until Judea was conquered by the Babylonians in 586 B.C.E. The Temple was rebuilt seventy years later, following the return of some Jews from Babylonian exile, and sacrifices were resumed. The Second Temple was greatly expanded by King Herod in the first century B.C.E.; it was destroyed by the Romans in 70 C.E.

Tikkun olam: Literally, "repairing the world." The obligation, incumbent upon Jews, to be God's partners in assuming the moral and ethical responsibilities that will make the world a more perfect and just place.

Torah: The Five Books of Moses, or Pentateuch, comprising the first section of the Hebrew Bible. Also used more generally to refer to Jewish learning and Jewish texts.

Tosefta: A collection of rabbinic teachings from the time of the Mishnah that was not included in it.

Written Torah: Another way of referring to the Five Books of Moses, or Pentateuch.

NOTES

Introduction

1. The one nondescendant of Hillel in this line of succession was Rabban Yochanan ben Zakkai, Hillel's great disciple. See the listing of Hillel's descendants in Rabbi Yisrael Meir Lau, *Rav Lau on Pirkei Avos*, p. 95.

1. Hillel, the Most Ardent of Students

1. At the heart of *The Book and the Sword*, Talmudic scholar Professor David Weiss Halivni's memoir of his Holocaust experiences, is the story of how he once spotted a Nazi concentration camp guard eating a greasy sandwich wrapped in a page of the *Shulchan Arukh*, the sixteenth-century code of Jewish law. Weiss Halivni was extremely moved by seeing this page, which brought back powerful memories of his Jewish learning in Hungary.

> "I instinctively fell at the feet of the guard, without even realizing why; the mere letters propelled me. With tears in my eyes, I implored him to give me this *bletl*, this page. For a while he didn't know what was happening. . . . He immediately put his hand to his revolver, the usual reaction to an unknown situation. But then he understood. This was, I explained to him, a page from a book I had studied at home. Please, I sobbed, give it to me as a souvenir. He gave me the *bletl* and I took it back to the camp. . . . The *bletl* became a rallying point. We looked forward to studying it whenever we had free time.

Like Hillel, Weiss Halivni risked his life to study Jewish holy texts because it wasn't worth living without them (see David Weiss Halivni, *The Book and the Sword: A Life of Learning in the Shadow of Destruction*, pp. 67–72).

2. Hillel's Rise to Leadership

1. A century later, the Idumeans participated actively in the 66–70 C.E. Jewish revolt against Rome. Most of them sided with the Zealots, the most nationalist and militant of the Jewish rebels. During Titus's siege of Jerusalem, the Idumeans formed a special division of about five thousand soldiers, and the Roman general Titus regarded them as an important element in the Jewish military forces (see *Encyclopaedia Judaica* 6:378). I mention this to underscore the point that, despite the inauspicious and very unfortunate way the Idumeans joined the Jewish people, many of them eventually developed a strong Jewish identity. Obviously, no Jew today has any way of knowing whether or not he or she possesses any Idumean ancestry, but at least some, perhaps many, Jews do.

2. Nahum N. Glatzer, *Hillel the Elder: The Emergence of Classical Judaism*.

3. Apparently, many years had passed since Passover had last fallen on a Friday night, and no one seemed to recall what had been done.

4. George Foot Moore, the early-twentieth-century Harvard historian of religion, argued that Hillel wanted to use logical principles to establish Jewish law, and not simply arguments from tradition, because arguments from logic allow Judaism to be more open to expansion and capable of being applied to new situations (see *Judaism in the First Centuries of the Christian Era*, pp. 78–81). To traditionalists, however, the argument from tradition is always the superior argument.

5. The Talmud elsewhere praises the Bnai Beteira for their humility in appointing Hillel over themselves (*Bava Metzia* 85a). Two centuries later, Hillel's descendant, Rabbi Judah the Prince, taught, "I am prepared to do whatever any person tells me except what the Bnai Beteira did for my ancestor [Hillel], in that they relinquished their high office

and promoted him to it" (*Genesis Rabbah* 33:3; see Judah Nadich's discussion of Rabbi Judah's statement in *Jewish Legends of the Second Commonwealth*, p. 202).

6. A virtually identical version of the story is recorded in the Jerusalem Talmud, *Pesachim* 6:1.

3. "While Standing on One Foot"

1. Edward M. Gershfield, "Hillel, Shammai, and the Three Proselytes," *Conservative Judaism*, 31, no. 3 (Spring 1967): 29–39.

2. The Torah's commandment—with its emphasis on "neighbor," implying a person whom we see often—suggests that this mitzvah relates to tangible behavior and not simply to abstract love, as would be the case had the Torah instructed us to "Love humanity." That is why Jewish legal texts generally focus on the actions this commandment entails. In the *Mishneh Torah*, Maimonides' fourteen-volume code of Jewish law, he describes as outgrowths of this command a series of additional Jewish laws (which are not specifically ordained in the Torah), including the commandments to visit the sick, to make sure that the dead are properly buried, to comfort mourners, to act hospitably, and to bring the bride and groom joy at their wedding. Maimonides understands the law of love of neighbor as meaning that whatever you want others to do for you, you should do for them ("Laws of Mourning" 14:1). In "Laws of Character Development," he offers additional examples of how to practice this commandment. For example: "One should speak in praise of another, and be careful about another's money [and possessions] just as he is careful about his own money, and wants his own dignity preserved" (6:3). These examples express two important components of loving behavior: emotional support for others (praising them) and material support (helping safeguard their money). In all the instances cited here, the commandment of love focuses on actions to be practiced, rather than on emotions felt internally.

4. Hillel and the Three Converts

1. In traditional Jewish law, a child of a convert is Jewish as long as the mother's conversion occurs prior to the child's birth. If the mother's conversion occurs subsequent to the birth, the child must undergo a separate conversion.

2. Even subsequent to Ruth's embracing the Israelite religion and peoplehood, the text speaks of her as "Ruth the Moabite" (Ruth 2:21), and one of Boaz's workers refers to her as "a Moabite girl" (Ruth 2:6), suggesting that many Israelites at the time might not have been fully open to conversion. Hence, the stunning power of the story's denouement, as the text reveals that this "Moabite girl" is the ancestress of Israel's greatest king.

3. Some Jews think it is, given that for so much of Jewish history, Judaism had little status and very few non-Jews expressed interest in converting. But in the Talmudic era, Jews were very open to influencing non-Jews with teachings from Judaism. The Jewish historian Josephus wrote in the first century: "The masses have long since shown a keen desire to adopt our religious observances, and there is not one city, Greek or barbarian, nor a single nation, to which our customs of abstaining from work on the seventh day has not spread, and where the fasts and lighting of [Sabbath] lamps and many of our prohibitions in the matter of food are not observed" (*Contra Apion* 2:39). Judaism had apparently become so highly regarded among segments of the Roman intelligentsia that Juvenal, the great Roman writer, composed a satire about Roman fathers who eat no pork, observe the Sabbath, worship only the heavenly God, and whose sons undergo circumcision, despise Roman laws, and study the Jews' Torah. Yet a third example: The New Testament, in a passage highly critical of the Jewish religious leadership, nonetheless states that Jews would "sail the seas and cross whole countries to win one convert" (Matthew 23:15).

4. When Maimonides published the *Mishneh Torah*, his code of Jewish law, his intention was to compose a book that would guide Jews on how to behave in all situations just by reading the Torah and his code. Needless to say, this provocative motivation outraged Jews who felt

that Maimonides was trying to obviate the study of Talmud, a work that cannot be replaced by a summary of the judgments it contains, or by any extraction of basic laws and principles. Three leading rabbis in France, outraged as well by Maimonides' religiously rationalist approach (reflected both in sections of the *Mishneh Torah* and in his *Guide for the Perplexed*) denounced his writings to the Dominicans, who headed the French Inquisition, and who were only too happy to burn Maimonides' books. And Maimonides was the greatest sage of the medieval period. Now imagine a first-century Gentile asking to be given the essence of an already ancient religion as if it were a pill he might swallow. No wonder Shammai was so outraged.

5. The Jewish sect known as the Karaites, generally distinguished by being biblical literalists, did not deduce from the words of the Shema the requirement ordained by the rabbis, and imposed no obligation on its adherents to wear tefillin.

6. In truth, as well known as the figure 613 is, the Torah never explicitly says that the Torah contains 613 laws. That figure appears in the Talmud (*Makkot* 23b), and serves as the basis for several major medieval works that delineated the commandments, most notably, Maimonides' *Sefer Ha-Mitzvot* (*The Book of the Commandments*) and *Sefer Ha-Chinnuch* (*The Book of Education*), which records the commandments—along with a commentary—in order of their appearance in the Torah.

7. Supposedly in line with the three instances in which Naomi told Ruth to "turn back" and not accompany her on her return to Israel. It was only after Ruth pleaded with Naomi yet a fourth time that Naomi "ceased to argue with her" (Ruth 1:6–18).

5. Repairing the World

1. Still others made loans and, when the poor couldn't pay back the money, sold off the debtor's children as slaves. There is evidence from the Bible itself that such mistreatment of the poor took place. A woman, a widow of a pious man, appeals to the prophet Elisha for immediate assistance because the creditor to whom she is indebted "is coming to take my two children to be his slaves" (2 Kings 4:1). In this

ninth century B.C.E. incident, Elisha performs a miracle that enables the woman to produce and sell sufficient quantities of cooking oil to repay her debt. The story is very beautiful and moving, but we can only imagine how many people who had no access to miracles had their children taken from them and enslaved. About a century later, the prophet Amos refers to some sort of immoral stratagem directed against the poor by which the "needy [are sold] for a pair of shoes" (Amos 2:6).

2. In Christian theology, Paul concluded that the laws of the Torah ultimately were a curse, since they could never be perfectly carried out, and Jews would be damned for any violation of any Torah law: "Those who rely on the keeping of the Law are under a curse, since Scripture says, 'Cursed be everyone who does not persevere in observing everything prescribed in the book of the Law [that is, the Torah]' " (see Gal. 3:10). Paul believed, therefore, that humankind must be redeemed from the law, a redemption that can come only through belief in Jesus: "Christ redeemed us from the curse of the Law" (Gal. 3:10). Elsewhere, Paul wrote, "We conclude that a man is put right with God only through faith and not by doing what the Law commands" (Rom. 3:28). Such a teaching flies in the face of the teaching of Jesus cited elsewhere, "Do not imagine that I have come to abolish the Law . . ." (Matt. 5:17; see p. 132). The Pauline idea that a person is cursed by God for breaking any law is a new one, and not found in the Hebrew Bible or in normative Jewish teachings. Hundreds of years before Paul, the Jews were assured that God recognizes that "there is no man so righteous who does only good and never sins" (Eccles. 7:20), and the Bible itself repeatedly tells of Jews who sinned (including Moses and David) and who—after repenting and returning to observance of the law—were restored to God's grace, certainly without being eternally cursed (see Dennis Prager and Joseph Telushkin, *The Nine Questions People Ask About Judaism*, pp. 78–83).

3. Even when one's life is at stake, it is still forbidden to murder an innocent person, engage in sexual offenses such as incest (see *Yoma* 82a; this does not mean, however, that a victim of incest rape should put her life at risk by resisting), and practice idolatry. It is not fully clear, though, when this last law applies. Rabbi Ishmael rules that if one is told, "Engage in idol worship so that you will not be killed," one should

comply with the demand as long as the act is not done in the presence of ten or more adult Jews, a minyan (see *Sanhedrin* 74a). Other rabbis command a Jew to martyr himself even if the only other person present is the idolater issuing the threat. Rabbi Ishmael's ruling strikes me as more compelling. Why would God prefer that a good person die when no irrevocable evil will ensue (as would be the case if one killed an innocent person to save one's life)? Surely the world will not be a better place if the good person is martyred while the idolater who murders him continues to live; indeed, it seems to me that the world will become a worse place.

4. For more examples of *tikkun olam* (and its outgrowth, *darkei shalom*, to achieve peace), see Mishnah *Gittin* 4:2–7, 5:3, and 5:8–9. In one uncommon instance, *Gittin* 4:5, the School of Shammai cites the principle of *tikkun olam* in the course of an argument with the School of Hillel, and Hillel's disciples recant and accept Shammai's ruling (see pp. 110–11).

6. Five Traits

1. Judges 14:10–20 tells of a bet Samson made with thirty men, which had tragic results.

2. Given that Hillel was himself from Babylonia, the question might well have been intended not only to waste Hillel's time, but as an insult (see Michael Katz and Gershon Schwartz, *Searching for Meaning in Midrash*, p. 139).

3. Adin Steinsaltz, *Talmudic Images*, p. 10.

4. Elie Wiesel, *Sages and Dreamers*, p. 168.

5. There are two instances in rabbinic literature in which Hillel expresses annoyance; see pp. 15–16.

6. Two comments on this story: "The same Hillel who taught that having servants can only cause trouble ["the more servant girls the more promiscuity, the more man-servants the more theft"; *Ethics of the Fathers* 2:7] took it upon himself to give this man what he was accustomed to, even though he himself considered it of little value" (Jonathan Duker, *The Spirits Behind the Law*, p. 77). "This story . . .

emphasizes his understanding that respect and honor are as essential for some people as food and drink are to others. Hillel, who himself was able to manage with very little, undarstood that others lived by different standards" (Adin Steinsaltz, *Talmudic Images*, p. 8).

7. I am indebted for this point to Danny Siegel.

8. I first came across this idea in the writings of Miriam Adahan, author of, among other books, *"Nobody's Perfect": Maintaining Emotional Health*, but I cannot locate where in her books I first found this idea.

7. Hillel the Interpreter, Shammai the Literalist

1. In some editions of the Tosefta, it is *Yoma* 5:2. The text doesn't record who it was who ordered him to feed his son more generously. Another text roots Shammai's behavior in his belief that the general prohibition on washing one's hands on Yom Kippur should not be suspended to feed a child (most parents of small children would wash at least one hand before feeding them). However, the rabbis, fearing that handing over food with unwashed hands could endanger a child's health, ordered Shammai to wash both hands and to feed the child with both. That, at least, is my understanding of a somewhat obscure text in *Yoma* 77b.

8. Thieves, Brides, and When Lying Is a Virtue

1. Of course, it was not necessarily only a sense of literalism that shaped Shammai's reasoning. Professor Louis Ginzberg (1873–1953), the great Talmudic scholar of the Jewish Theological Seminary, rooted many of the disagreements between Hillel and Shammai and their schools in socioeconomic issues. Shammai, he argued, consistently ruled in accordance with the interests and practices of wealthier Jews, whereas Hillel's rulings favored the interests and practices of poorer ones (the position discussed elsewhere, that the School of Shammai advocated restricting access to higher Jewish education to "the rich," already suggests such a bias; see pp. 145–47). Similarly, you would have to have an innate sensitivity to society's poorer elements (rather than a

commitment to the "letter of the law") to recognize that demanding of a penitent thief that he destroy his home will likely destroy any chance that the person will repent. While Ginzberg, I believe, does not discuss this particular case, he does cite several other Hillel/Shammai conflicts in support of his thesis. For example, the School of Hillel requires a blessing over bread at the beginning of a meal (*ha-motzi*), following which, even if other foods are eaten, no additional blessing is required. The School of Shammai rules that the blessing over bread covers the bread and only the bread; all other dishes require their own blessing. Superficially, one might argue that the Shammaites were more punctilious in their ritual observances and searched out additional opportunities to bless and thank God. Ginzberg offers an altogether different rationale: "The reason for their disagreement was that bread was the main dish of a poor man's meal and, therefore, once he recited a benediction over it, he thereby blessed the entire meal. For the rich man, however, who ate meat, fish, and all kinds of delicacies, bread was not the main dish. The School of Shammai consequently maintained that even cooked foods were not included in a benediction over bread" (Louis Ginzberg, *On Jewish Law and Lore*, p. 104; the discussion of the impact of economic factors in the variant rulings between the two schools is found on pp. 102–18). What strikes me as a counterargument to that offered by Ginzberg is the Mishnah in *Gittin* 4:5, in which the School of Hillel favors slave owners, while the School of Shammai favors the slaves (see pages 109–11 in this book). Consistent with the thesis offered in this volume, Ginzberg attributed many other disputes between the schools to Shammai's emphasis on fulfilling the precise acts ordained by the Torah, and to Hillel's greater emphasis on the significance of intention: "The School of Shammai . . . considered deed more important than thought . . . as over against the progressive view of the School of Hillel who taught that an act not accompanied by intention is not to be considered an act" (Ginzberg, *On Jewish Law and Lore*, p. 119). Professor Shmuel Safrai has challenged Ginzberg's socioeconomic explanation of the Hillel/Shammai disputes and notes that we only have information about the economic status of four disciples, two of each school's. "About Rabbi Eliezer it is stated that he was in fact rich, as opposed to Rabbi Joshua ben Chananiah, the representative of the

House of Hillel, who was extremely poor. However, of the other two . . . the Shammaite Rabbi Yochanan ben He-Horanit was very poor, while Rabbi Tzadok of [the School of Hillel] was apparently rich," and sent food to Rabbi Yochanan when he heard about his poverty (Shmuel Safrai, ed., *The Literature of the Sages*, p. 188).

2. For a further, more nuanced analysis of this debate, see the Midrashic text *Kallah Rabbati* 10:1.

3. The Tosafot commentary on the Talmud argues that Shammai intended people to praise the bride, but to confine their praise to those features that were truly attractive, for example, "her eyes or hands if they are pretty." If this is correct, it still makes sense why Hillel advocated a general, though sometimes untruthful, formula for praising all brides. If wedding guests restricted their praise to one or two features, it might well have the effect of reminding everyone of the bride's less attractive, though unmentioned, features.

4. Perhaps, one might argue, in contrast to both Hillel and Shammai, if one thinks the bride unattractive, it would be better to say nothing at all. Indeed, a later Talmudic commentator, the Maharam Schiff, raises the question of why, in such a case, the wedding guests don't simply remain silent about the woman's looks. Doing so, the rabbi writes, "would be repulsive," since other brides are praised for their beauty. When was the last time you attended a wedding in which you didn't hear people tell the bride, "You look so beautiful." Therefore, saying nothing about the bride's appearance is in effect the same as calling her unattractive, though obviously saying so outright would be worse.

10. Shammai Beyond Stereotype

1. The price he asks for is 400 shekels of silver. The book of Jeremiah, written many hundreds of years later (ca. 600 B.C.E.), records that a small plot of land, likely comparable in size to the plot sold Abraham, was sold for 17 shekels of silver (Jer. 32:9).

2. As Judah Nadich explains, once Yonatan came into legal possession of the property, "it was his to do with as he liked, and he therefore was not violating the deceased's wishes for it was not the latter's prop-

erty Yonatan gave to the sons, but his own" (Judah Nadich, ed., *Jewish Legends of the Second Commonwealth*, p. 229 n. 90). The above citation is not the precise and tersely worded response offered by Yonatan; I have basically followed Nadich's summary of the event.

3. It is possible, though the biblical text does not say this, that Uriah heard rumors in the palace of the king's clandestine affair with his wife (David had had Bathsheba brought to him), and that is why he refused to go home to be with her.

4. Though it does correspond to the "letter of the law," as understood by the biblical prophet Nathan.

11. Two Torahs

1. In the first case, Shammai rules that a menstruating woman is *tamei* (the opposite of a state of purity, and therefore forbidden to be in physical contact with her husband) from the time she discovers a discharge of blood, while Hillel regards the woman as *tamei* starting with the last time she had examined herself. In the second instance, Shammai rules that challah, a dough offering, must be separated from a portion of dough containing at least one *kav* (a measurement equal to the volume of twenty-four eggs) of flour, while Hillel rules that it is to be taken from two *kavs* of flour. In the third case, Shammai rules that if a mikvah contains nine *kavs* of drawn water, it becomes invalid for use, while Hillel rules that it becomes invalidated by a *hin* (three *kavs*) of drawn water. Ironically, and despite Shammai's reputation for strictness and Hillel's for leniency, Hillel's view is the more stringent in the first and third of the three cases.

2. Shmuel Safrai, ed., *The Literature of the Sages*, p. 186.

3. Ibid., p. 191.

4. In nine instances, the School of Hillel deferred to the School of Shammai (see, for examples, pp. 99–100 and 109–11), and in several cases, the law does not follow either (see, as noted, *Eduyot* 1:1–3). Professor Safrai argues that there isn't a single instance of the School of Shammai accepting a view of the School of Hillel, though the commentary on the Mishnah, *Tiferet Yisrael*, argues that *Terumot* 5:4 seems to indicate

an acceptance by the School of Shammai of a ruling of the School of Hillel; see also, Herbert Danby, *The Mishnah*, p. 58, n. 3).

5. The *Ethics of the Fathers* contrasts the high-minded disputes of Hillel and Shammai with the self-aggrandizing behavior of Korach, who challenged and tried to overthrow Moses in the desert (Num., chap. 16). The disagreements of Hillel and Shammai are referred to as "a dispute for the sake of heaven" because the disputants were motivated by the desire to find truth; no personal benefit accrued to them if their position was accepted (that is why it was easier for the disputants to generally remain on friendly terms). In contrast, Korach, as depicted in the Torah, was driven by the desire for personal gain, in his case, power. As regards those few instances in which the law does not follow the teachings of either Hillel or Shammai, the Mishnah asks why their opinions are therefore cited, since they will not be followed. The answer? "So as to teach generations to come that a person should not hold stubbornly to his opinions, for the fathers of the world (that is, Hillel and Shammai) did not hold stubbornly to their opinions" (*Eduyot* 1:4).

6. See Safrai, *Literature of the Sages*, p. 196.

12. The Jewish Sage and the Christian Messiah

1. This was a decision that paved the way for large-scale conversions to Christianity. It was, for example, much easier for males to accept a new faith that did not require them to be circumcised. Jesus' earlier followers, headed by his brother, James, insisted, in conformity with Jesus, that Torah laws were still binding. The New Testament book of Acts (10:14) notes that Peter, whom Catholics regard as the first pope, kept kosher. Acts 2:46 and 3:1 record that Jesus' disciples regularly prayed at the Jerusalem Temple (which, by the way, would have been very unlikely if they believed the Jews responsible for crucifying Jesus). James sent out emissaries to teach that the law of circumcision still applied (Acts 15:1; see also Gal. 2:12), and he also ordered Paul to observe Jewish laws (Acts 21:24). Paul, however, rejected James's command: "We conclude," he taught instead, "that a man is put right with God only through faith and not by doing what the Law commands" (Rom. 3:28).

It was Paul's, not James's, teachings that prevailed in Christianity. Paul's opposition to Torah law was basic to his theology. If it was true, as Judaism taught, that observing the Torah's laws could make one righteous in God's eyes, then that would mean that people could achieve righteousness through their own efforts. And if that were so, Paul reasoned, there was no need for Jesus, no purpose to the Crucifixion, and "Christ would have died in vain" (Gal. 2:21). Once Paul marginalized the Torah's law and dropped the legal requirements for converting to Judaism, Christianity ceased being a Jewish sect and became a separate religion. As I have noted elsewhere, "From the perspective of Christianity, this made Paul into a great hero, Saint Paul. Most Jews find it hard to regard him with equal adulation" (Joseph Telushkin, *Jewish Literacy*, p. 126).

2. The first half of the citation is from Hyam Maccoby's *The Mythmaker*, p. 24, and the second half is from his *Early Rabbinic Writings*, p. 62.

13. "Teach Everyone"

1. One of the great works of modern Jewish literature, *As a Driven Leaf*, is an attempt by Rabbi Milton Steinberg to comprehend what could have driven so great a rabbi to become so great an enemy of his people. Despite Elisha's cooperation with the Romans, Steinberg regards Elisha as more tragic than evil, a man alienated from Judaism on intellectual grounds who ultimately becomes alienated from Roman philosophy and culture on both intellectual and moral grounds, and ends his life as a broken, utterly lonely man, believing in nothing.

2. Adin Steinsaltz, *Talmudic Images*, p. 11.

14. "The Highly Impatient Person Cannot Teach": For Today's Teachers and Parents

1. The same passage also frees from punishment a father who kills his son while disciplining him. Technically, the discussion simply exonerates such a person from enforced exile to "a city of refuge," the punish-

ment for "a manslayer who has killed a person unintentionally" (see Num. 35:9–15). However, the rabbinic discussion of this ruling makes it clear that no punishment was inflicted as long as the father (or teacher) could argue that the punishment was inflicted "to incline the child in a different [better] path" (Rashi on *Makkot* 8a).

2. So serious is the crime of humiliating another that the Talmud declares, "Whoever shames his neighbor in public, it is as if he shed his blood" (*Bava Metzia* 58b). The rabbis go on to say that one who shames another in public forfeits his or her place in the world to come (*Bava Metzia* 59a). Fortunately, given that most of us have been guilty of this offense at least once, Maimonides teaches that such punishment is exacted only from those who routinely engage in such behavior ("Laws of Repentance" 3:14). Furthermore, this prohibition applies to humiliating children as strongly as it applies to adults (*Bava Kamma* 86a–b). Indeed, children are more vulnerable than adults to all kinds of attacks, including humiliation. The guiding principle for teachers should be the words of *Ethics of the Fathers:* "Let the honor of your students be as dear to you as your own" (*Ethics of the Fathers* 4:12). My friend Rabbi David Woznica comments that "since the most important teachers in a child's life are his or her parents, this lesson, that 'the highly impatient person cannot teach,' is particularly important for parents as well."

15. "One Who Is Bashful Will Never Learn"

1. See pp. 12–16 re Bnai Beteira.

2. Adin Steinsaltz, *Talmudic Images*, p. 126.

3. See Norman Lamm, "Knowing vs. Learning: Which Takes Precedence?" in Susan Handelman and Jeffrey Saks, *Wisdom from All My Teachers*, p. 18 n. 7.

18. Final Thoughts

1. Deuteronomy 22:10 prohibits plowing one's field with animals of unequal strength (e.g., an ox and a donkey) harnessed together; Deuteronomy 25:4 forbids muzzling an animal while it is working in the

field, and thereby preclude the creature from eating; Leviticus 22:28 prohibits slaughtering an animal and its young at the same time. The widely accepted *Sefer Ha-Chinukh*, a study of the Torah's 613 laws and their rationales that was published in thirteenth-century Spain, explains that the rules of ritual slaughter were intended "so that we don't cause too much suffering to the animal, for though the Torah permitted man . . . to use animals for food and for all his needs, it is forbidden to cause an animal needless pain" (Commandment #451).

Appendix 1. "He Who Does Not Increase, Will Decrease"

1. James David Weiss, *Vintage Wein*, pp. 213–16.

2. Hyam Maccoby, *Early Rabbinic Writings*, p. 125.

3. See my discussion of this topic in Joseph Telushkin, *Jewish Literacy*, p. 617.

4. The *ketubah* is signed by witnesses before the wedding ceremony, and following the ceremony the bride and groom are escorted to a closed room where they are secluded for about ten minutes. This procedure is known as *yichud* (separation), and it is a ceremony of great symbolic significance. Prior to marriage, traditional Jewish law forbids a man and woman who are not closely related to be alone in an inaccessible room. *Yichud*, then, is the final act in the wedding ceremony, indicating that the couple is now married and sexually permitted to each other.

Appendix 2. Hillel's Seven *Middot* of Torah Interpretation

1. I am indebted to the ArtScroll Siddur for its translation of, and commentary on, Rabbi Yishmael's thirteen rules of Torah interpretation (which include six of Hillel's principles), as well as to Philip Birnbaum's prayer book, *Ha-Siddur Ha-Shalem*, and to Yitzhak Frank's and Ezra Zion Melamed's *The Practical Talmud Dictionary*.

BIBLIOGRAPHY

A Note on Citations from Judaism's Classic Texts

When citing statements from the Hebrew Bible, the TaNaKh, I have generally relied upon the translation of the Jewish Publication Society (Philadelphia, 1985), a scholarly yet highly readable rendering of the Bible into contemporary English. On occasion, however, I have translated the verses myself, or used other translations that seemed to me preferable for a specific verse.

There are three English translations of the Mishnah, and the one on which I have relied most is Jacob Neusner's *The Mishnah* (New Haven, Conn.: Yale University Press, 1988). There is an older and still valuable translation of the Mishnah by Herbert Danby (Oxford: Clarendon Press, 1933). In addition, I have also frequently consulted Pinchas Kehati's excellent Hebrew commentary on the entire Mishnah, *Mishnayot Mevuarot* (Jerusalem: Heichal Shlomo, 1977), which has been translated into English as well (Jerusalem: Department for Torah Education and Culture in the Diaspora of the World Zionist Organization, 1988). I have also consulted Jacob Neusner's two-volume translation, *The Tosefta* (Peabody, Mass.: Hendrickson Publishers, 2002).

The citations from *Pirkei Avot (Ethics of the Fathers)*, which is a tractate within the Mishnah, are based on the enumeration within the Mishnah, which on occasion differs from the enumeration of *Pirkei Avot* as printed in the *siddur* (prayer book).

In quoting from the Talmud, I have for the most part relied on the ArtScroll translation, one of the great works of modern Jewish literature. ArtScroll, which is based in Brooklyn, New York, has in recent years completed a translation into English of the entire Babylonian Talmud* along with extensive explanatory notes. The ArtScroll edition is a line-by-line translation, and anyone who has Hebrew skills can utilize this translation to learn the Talmud's basic vocabulary and methodology. I have also consulted the highly accurate and literal translation of the Soncino Press (London, 1935), and the Hebrew translation and commentary of Rabbi Adin Steinsaltz on the Talmud. In addition, Random House has brought out many volumes of Steinsaltz's Talmud into English, in a very readable translation (under titles such as *The Talmud, The Steinsaltz Edition, Volume 1: Bava Mezia Part I*). Although I have repeatedly consulted these works, I have also translated many of the cited texts myself.

Yale University Press has published Judah Goldin's translation of *The Fathers According to Rabbi Nathan* (1955).

The citations from the *Midrash Rabbah* have primarily fol-

---

* When people speak of studying Talmud, they almost always mean the Babylonian Talmud, and not the shorter and earlier Jerusalem Talmud. In any case, ArtScroll has now started publishing a translation and commentary on the Jerusalem Talmud as well.

lowed the Soncino translation (London, 1983: ten volumes), although I have checked all translations against the original, and have often made some alterations.

Yale University Press has published a multivolume translation of almost all of Moses Maimonides' *Mishneh Torah* under the title, *The Code of Maimonides.* In recent years, Rabbi Eliyahu Touger has been bringing out a very readable translation of Maimonides' *Mishneh Torah*, with the Hebrew and English on facing pages (the set is not yet complete). In addition, Rabbi Touger provides extensive notes on Maimonides' text, and also cites the Talmudic and other sources for Maimonides' rulings (the work is published by the New York–based Moznaim Publishing Corporation). I have also relied on the Hebrew-language edition of the *Mishneh Torah* by the Mossad Ha-Rav Kook publishing house (Jerusalem), which contains the wide-ranging commentary of Rabbi Shmuel Tanchum Rubenstein.

The other Hebrew works that are cited are listed, along with the other books I consulted, in the following bibliography.

Adahan, Miriam. *Nobody's Perfect: Maintaining Emotional Health.* Nanuet, N.Y.: Feldheim Publishers, 1994.

Berkovits, Eliezer. *Not in Heaven: The Nature and Function of Halakha.* New York: Ktav Publishing, 1983.

Birnbaum, Philip. *Daily Prayer Book*, *Ha-Siddur Ha-Shalem.* Whitefish, Mont.: Kessinger Publishing, 2007.

Buxbaum, Yitzchak. *The Life and Teachings of Hillel.* Northvale, N.J.: Jason Aronson, 1994.

Bibliography

Charlesworth, James, and Loren Johns, eds. *Hillel and Jesus: Comparisons of Two Major Religious Leaders.* Minneapolis: Fortress Press, 1997.

Cohen, Shaye. *The Beginnings of Jewishness: Boundaries, Varieties, Uncertainties.* Berkeley, Calif.: University of California Press, 2001.

Duker, Rabbi Jonathan. *The Spirits Behind the Law: The Talmudic Scholars.* New York: Urim Publications, 2007.

Epstein, Lawrence, ed. *Readings on Conversion to Judaism.* Northvale, N.J.: Mason Aronson, 1995.

Feldman, Emanuel, and Joel B. Wolowelsky. *The Conversion Crisis: Essays from the Pages of Tradition.* New York: Ktav Publishing, 1990.

Feldman, Louis. *Jew and Gentile in the Ancient World.* Princeton, N.J.: Princeton University Press, 1996.

Fine, Howard, and Chris Freeman. *Fine on Acting: A Vision of the Craft.* West Hollywood, Calif.: Havenhurst Books, 2009.

Flusser, David. *Judaism of the Second Temple Period* Vol. 2, *The Jewish Sages and Their Literature.* Translated by Azzan Yadin. Grand Rapids, Mich.: William B. Eerdmans Publishing Company, 2009.

Frank, Yitzchak, and Ezra Zion Melamed. *The Practical Talmud Dictionary.* Jerusalem: Ariel United Israel Institutions, 1992.

Gilat, Y. D. *R. Eliezer ben Hyrcanus: A Scholar Outcast.* Ramat Gan, Israel: Bar-Ilan University Press, 1984.

Ginzberg, Louis. *On Jewish Law and Lore.* New York: Atheneum, 1970.

Glatzer, Nahum N. *Hillel the Elder: The Emergence of Classical Judaism.* New York: Schocken Books, 1956.

Halivni, David Weiss. *The Book and the Sword: A Life of Learning in the Shadow of Destruction.* New York: Westview Press, 1997.

Handelman, Susan, and Jeffrey Saks. *Wisdom From All My Teachers: Challenges and Initiatives in Contemporary Torah Eduction.* Jerusalem: Urim Publications, 2003.

Katz, Michael, and Gershon Schwartz. *Searching for Meaning in Midrash.* Philadelphia: Jewish Publication Society, 2002.

Konovitz, Rabbi Dr. Israel. *Beit Shammai and Beit Hillel* (Hebrew). Jerusalem: Mossad Harav Kook, 1965.

Lau, Rabbi Yisrael Meir. *Rav Lau on Pirkei Avos.* Vol. 1, *A Comprehensive Commentary on* Ethics of the Fathers. Adapted by Yaacov Dovid Shulman. Brooklyn, N.Y.: Mesorah Publications, 2006.

Maccoby, Hyam. *Early Rabbinic Writings.* New York: Cambridge University Press, 1988.

———. *The Mythmaker: Paul and the Invention of Christianity.* New York: Barnes and Noble Books, 1998.

Miller, Chaim. *Chumash: The Gutnick Edition.* Brooklyn, N.Y.: Kol Menachem, 2008.

Moore, George Foot. *Judaism in the First Centuries of the Christian Era.* Cambridge, Mass.: Harvard University Press, 1962.

Nadich, Judah. *Jewish Legends of the Second Commonwealth.* Philadelphia: Jewish Publication Society, 1983.

Prager, Dennis, and Joseph Telushkin. *The Nine Questions Peo-*

ple Ask About Judaism. New York: Touchstone Press, 1986.

Rubenstein, Jeffrey L. *Rabbinic Stories.* New York: Paulist Press, 2002.

Safrai, Shmuel, ed. *The Literature of the Sages: First Part: Oral Tora, Halakha, Mishna, Tosefta, Talmud, External Tractates.* Philadelphia: Van Gorcum, Fortress Press, 1987.

Scherman, Nosson. *The ArtScroll Siddur.* Brooklyn, N.Y.: ArtScroll, 1987.

Sperber, Daniel. *A Commentary on Derech Erez Zuta: Chapters Five to Eight.* Ramat Gan, Israel: Bar-Ilan University Press, 1990.

Steinsaltz, Adin. *Talmudic Images.* Northvale, N.J.: Jason Aronson Inc., 1997.

Telushkin, Joseph. *Jewish Literacy.* Rev. ed. New York: William Morrow, 2008.

Urbach, Ephraim. *Collected Writings in Jewish Studies.* Jerusalem: The Hebrew University Magnes Press, 1999.

————. *The Halakhah: Its Sources and Development.* Jerusalem: Yad La Talmud, 1986.

Walzer, Michael, Menachem Lorberbaum, and Noam J. Zohar, eds. *The Jewish Political Tradition.* Vol. 1, *Authority.* New Haven, Conn.: Yale University Press, 2000.

Weiss, James David. *Vintage Wein: The Collected Wit and Wisdom, the Choicest Anecdotes and Vignettes of Rabbi Berel Wein.* Brooklyn, N.Y.: Shaar Press, 1992.

Wiesel, Elie. *Sages and Dreamers: Biblical, Talmudic, and Hasidic Portraits and Legends.* New York: Summit Books, 1991.

ACKNOWLEDGMENTS

The pleasantest part of finishing a book is having the opportunity to publicly acknowledge those who helped—in this case profoundly helped—me in the writing of this book.

I have been blessed throughout my writing career with a number of remarkable editors, but the level of vision and extraordinarily concrete suggestions offered me by Jonathan Rosen has been an experience I will always cherish (and look forward to repeating). Not only did Jonathan's vision of the book largely parallel my own, but he forced me to open my eyes and mind much wider, and to really underscore why Hillel matters as much to our century as he did to his own. Jonathan's level of knowledge and insight about a subject on which he himself was not writing staggers me, and I cannot overstate how much he improved this book.

It is by now a commonplace to acknowledge Carolyn Hessel as a, perhaps *the*, primal force in the promotion of Jewish reading and Jewish books today in the United States—and increasingly beyond the borders of the United States. But I am writing of Carolyn here as a friend, a person whose friendship has immeasurably blessed my life. She combines equal doses of warmth, loyalty, intelligence, and absolute bluntness, and not just to me but to the whole Telushkin family, and to so many others. She has turned the making of friends into an art. And in addition to all her other commitments, she also gave this book a very careful and repeatedly helpful reading.

My dear friend Rabbi Israel "Izzy" Stein reviewed all the references cited in this book. Izzy has taught me over the years that checking all of a writer's footnotes is one of the best ways to understand how the writer has developed his book's thesis and conclusions. This was a painstaking job, and I am indebted to Rabbi Stein for his blessed help, as well as for his numerous suggestions.

Six beloved friends, Dr. Isaac Herschkopf, Rabbi David Woznica, Rabbi Irwin Kula, Professor Michael Berger, Rabbi Saul Berman, and Daniel Taub, read this work in manuscript and offered me a myriad challenges and improvements. I cannot imagine finishing this book without the aid of the measured, and sometimes critical, readings these friends offered me. I have had the honor to write about the help extended to me by each of these friends at greater length in the acknowledgments to *A Code of Jewish Ethics*, volumes 1 and 2. I feel particularly blessed to have these insights come from people who have collectively been dear friends for over a hundred and fifty years. Professor Steven Cohen, the preeminent sociologist of American Jewish life and a friend dating back to our days as graduate students at Columbia University, reviewed for me the statistical data and also directed me to the best sources to verify other statements. I am very grateful. I would also like to thank Rabbi Marc Angel whose writings first brought to my attention the responsa of the late Chief Rabbi Ben-Zion Uziel.

I also wish to acknowledge the book's very first reader, my

daughter Shira. An increasingly erudite Talmudist, Shira went over this manuscript with me several times, including a full two-hour conversation with her on Skype at Yeshivat Migdal Oz, where she was studying in Israel. Chapter after chapter, she improved this book.

My wife Dvorah, a great supporter of this project, constantly goaded me to develop the theme of Hillel's openness to conversion and to welcoming people into the Jewish community, a subject that has become so important at this time, a full two thousand years since Hillel's passing.

I also want to acknowledge and thank the rest of my family: Rebecca, Naomi, and Benjamin, who have patiently and tolerantly heard me expound, perhaps more than they wished, on the wisdom and importance of Hillel, and always gave me a supportive hearing.

I am pleased as well to thank David Szonyi. By this time, I have lost count of how many of my books David has worked on, but he has been editing me since *Jewish Literacy*, and I owe so much to his stylistic and editorial improvements.

I am honored to thank as well Altie Karper, the deservedly renowned editor of Schocken Books. The writing of this book has fulfilled a long-standing ambition to publish a book with Altie, and her editing has been painstaking and extremely helpful.

I am grateful as well for the very careful copyediting done by Muriel Jorgensen, whose work convinced me that even after one is sure that editing has been completed it hasn't been, and for the wonderful glossary compiled and defined by Rahel Lerner.

Acknowledgments

There have been a number of books written on Hillel—surprisingly not that many given his significance—and I want to express my appreciation in particular to Rabbi Dr. Israel Konovitz, editor of *Beit Shammai v'Beit Hillel*, a compilation in the original Hebrew and Aramaic of every statement of Hillel and Shammai, and of the schools of Hillel and Shammai, in the Talmudic literature, and to Rabbi Yitzhak Buxbaum, author of *The Life and Teachings of Hillel*, a comprehensive compilation and highly insightful commentary on Hillel's teachings. I also wish to acknowledge Nahum Glatzer, author of *Hillel the Elder: The Emergence of Classical Judaism*. I am indebted as well to the many scholarly books and articles cited within.

ABOUT THE AUTHOR

Joseph Telushkin is the author of sixteen books, including *Jewish Literacy*, *The Book of Jewish Values*, and *A Code of Jewish Ethics*, the first volume of which received a National Jewish Book Award in 2006. He is a Senior Associate of The National Jewish Center for Learning and Leadership (CLAL), serves on the board of the Jewish Book Council, and is the rabbi of the Synagogue for the Performing Arts in Los Angeles. He lectures throughout the United States and lives in New York City.